A HISTORY OF
QUEEN'S COLLEGE, LONDON

A HISTORY OF QUEEN'S COLLEGE, LONDON 1848–1972

By

ELAINE KAYE

1972
CHATTO & WINDUS
LONDON

Published by
Chatto & Windus Ltd
40 William IV Street
London WC2N 4DF
*
Clarke, Irwin & Co. Ltd
Toronto

ISBN 0 7011 1876 8

Printed in Great Britain by
Cox & Wyman Ltd,
London, Fakenham and Reading

CONTENTS

ILLUSTRATIONS

FOREWORD

I have many people to thank for their help in the writing of this history. First and above all I should like to thank Miss Ceridwen Oliver, the Registrar and Archivist of the College; she has throughout its progress given generous help and informed criticism. Secondly I should like to thank the Council of the College, and the Principal, Mrs Fierz, for generous co-operation and support.

I am also grateful to Miss Beatrice Burstall, Mrs Fierz, Miss Clare Lambert, Mrs Meg Parker and Dr Patricia Shaw for constructive criticism. I have to thank Mrs Fierz, Miss Holloway, Mrs Evelyn Murphy, Dr Shaw, Mrs Sprague and Miss Irene Swinford Edwards for sharing with me their reminiscences of Queen's. The following former students also helped by sending me their reminiscences of Queen's: Elayne Ancill (Finegold), Jane Borton (Smith), Sally Brompton, Bernice Burr (Harrison), Josephine Clark (Hollier), Hilary Coates, Frances Findlay (Willmott), Linda Haley, Bridget Levitt, Janet di Marco (Lewis), Ann Saville-Taylor, Gillian Schacht (Wormall), Diana Sparkes (Foss), Jenifer Williams (Cass), Jane Wilmot and Rosemary Yablon (Steel).

I should like to thank the Schoolmistresses and Governesses Benevolent Institution (formerly the G.B.I.) and its secretary, Mr J. W. Beattie, for permission to look at and quote from its papers and records. The Honourable Penelope Piercy kindly gave permission for Samuel Laurence's drawing of Maurice to be reproduced.

Finally I should also like to thank Mr Martin Lloyd and Mrs Elizabeth Morgan for their co-operation and my family for their never-failing help and encouragement.

Missenden Abbey. February 1972. ELAINE KAYE.

I
Foundation

ON April 20 1844, a dinner was held at the London Tavern, at which forty-seven 'noblemen and gentlemen' were present, under the chairmanship of the Duke of Cambridge. The guest speaker was a thirty-two-year-old writer with several novels already to his credit: Charles Dickens. Dickens was in great demand as a speaker at dinners on behalf of charitable institutions and had to refuse most of the invitations. But this one he had accepted, without hesitation. 'I should perform Lord Castlereagh's feat of turning my back on myself, if I hesitated for an Instant,' he replied.

The dinner was being held for the subscribers to the Governesses' Benevolent Institution, a recently established society enjoying the support of politicians, bishops and members of the aristocracy. The cause was a deserving one, and a previously neglected one. *The Morning Post*[1] reported Dickens' speech thus:

> It was very well to say that 'knowledge is power', but how often did they forget that it was a source of weakness too? (Applause). Knowledge had not its right place in society, and he believed that it did not obtain a just recognition and reward for its services anywhere. To take the case of those ladies in comparison with menial servants: they were worse paid than the cook; their salaries would bear poor comparison with the wages of the butler; they would appear but shabbily with the remuneration of the lady's maid; and they were even lower than those paid to liveried footmen. (Cheers). The power of governesses was acknowledged by the middle-aged lady in a turban—she felt the power of the governess' knowledge in the education of her

[1] April 22 1844

> daughters; gentlemen also felt the power of the governess' knowledge; but nobody thought of the poor fagged knowledge herself, her eyes red with poring over advertisements in search of a new situation; and after having faithfully accomplished her task in one family, being thrown upon the world, and going forth again among strangers to educate others . . .
>
> From first to last he had a confidence that the society would do its duty; and he hoped by its means to see blotted out a national reproach, and that the profession of education would be placed on that honourable footing which in any civilised and Christian land, it ought to hold.

This confidence in the future of the society's work was justified. The schemes initiated by the Governesses' Benevolent Institution contributed, during the following fifty years, to the whole development of secondary education for girls, and to the opening of the universities and of the professions to women.

No-one in 1844 could have foreseen these developments, for the aims and ambitions of the society were comparatively modest. It began first in 1829 as a Governesses' Mutual Assurance Society; this proved ineffective, since governesses were not in a position to save. In 1841, it was re-formed as the Governesses' Benevolent and Provident Institution, but its secretary proved unsatisfactory and little was done. In 1843 the society changed its name again to the Governesses' Benevolent Institution, and acquired the services of two men important to its future. One was David Laing, a clergyman interested in education, who became its efficient and effective secretary. His home, the Vicarage of Holy Trinity, St Pancras, was a meeting place for many of the literary figures of the day. Laing was deeply interested in the social and educational projects in which he was involved, and gave himself unsparingly to them. It did not unfortunately prevent him from showing touchiness at times, leading to awkward situations at Queen's later on. He was a friend of the Buss family in Camden Town, and gave Frances Mary Buss every encouragement, both to improve her own education and to establish the North London Collegiate School for Ladies (in 1850), of which he was a patron.

The other recruit was Frederick Denison Maurice, Professor of English Literature and Modern History at King's College, London, who joined the committee and attended its meetings regularly, his interest having stemmed from his sister's experience as a teacher and friend of governesses. He was of even more importance for the future educational work of the society.

The institution asked for subscriptions, from which it offered temporary help to governesses who had finished their task in one family but were young enough to look for another position, and provided a few annuities for governesses unable to continue working. There was immediately a long queue of applicants for help, and far more governesses were turned away than were offered help. In 1848, for example, ninety-five governesses applied for three annuities; all were subjected to the indignity of canvassing their names to the subscribers, and ninety-two were disappointed and left to ask for help wherever they could. This practice soon earned the society the disapproval of Dickens, its erstwhile supporter. In 1847 he wrote to David Laing:

> My objection to the Governesses Institution is increased every year. I think that canvassing is one of the social vices of this time; and am ashamed of possessing a vote, when I find so many reduced ladies driven to the necessity of seeking it in vain. It appears to me that there is an amount of degradation and humiliating solicitation imposed upon the candidates which is very poorly paid for, even in a successful instance, and which we are not justified in inflicting upon any class of persons, however willing they may be to undergo it.[1]

Grants, however, were more abundant, and more than half of the two hundred and fifty who applied in 1845, for example, were fortunate.

The governess was a special victim of Victorian society. Any

[1] Governesses' Papers I, p. 503, in the records of the G.B.I.

woman who was compelled to work had, by definition, no social status, for women were to be wives and mothers. Marriage was the accepted profession for the upper or middle-class woman, and there was no other. Victorian propriety ignored many things. One of them was the surplus of women over men; another was the comparatively high proportion of men who did not marry. The widow or unmarried woman left without private means sank into social oblivion in the only occupation open to her—that of the governess.

The *Quarterly Review*[1] defined the governess as 'a being who is our equal in birth, manner, and education, but our inferior in worldly wealth'. Mrs Anna Jameson, unusual in that she had been a governess herself for many years before her marriage and career as a writer, wrote in a remarkably sympathetic essay[2] on governesses (an effective contrast to some of the unctuous literature otherwise being written on the subject):

> With every advance in civilisation, the position of the instructor advances in importance and in dignity: how is it that precisely the reverse is the case where women are concerned? With them the task of education has ceased to have the sanctity and dignity of a religious calling; it has no rank as a profession; and it leads to nothing that I know of but a broken constitution, and a lonely unblessed old age.

Impossible demands were made of the governess, who was in any case ill-educated for her task. There were frequent advertisements for governesses in *The Times*, requiring extensive qualifications but offering no salary. *Punch*[3] suggested the following reply to a typical advertisement:

> Sir – Having a comfortable patrimony, and acknowledging that high and elevating necessity of our nature, that com-

[1] December 1848, vol. 84.
[2] In *Memoirs and Essays illustrative of art, literature and social morals* (1846).
[3] Vol. XV, p. 78.

pels the heart to love something, I should feel myself selected by the happiest fortune, did you think me worthy of fulfilling the serious, and no less delicious duties of Nursery Governess to your interesting children (number no consequence).

If I have any emotion in excess, it is that of the love of children; a quality, perhaps, only second to that of plain and ornamental needlework. My activity never permits me to have a moment's leisure; and my good temper, from the time of my infancy, has passed into a family proverb.

You state, Sir, and I admire the frankness—that 'no salary will be given'. I fully understand, Sir, that the delightful privilege of dwelling under your roof, and enjoying the pure moral atmosphere of your hearth, must exceed any value to be awarded by the coined dross of this selfish world. How happy am I that, possessing a sufficient competence of my own, I may give myself up heart, and soul, and pocket, to the formation of the minds of your children, and to the daily execution of your needlework. Deign, Sir, to consider my application with the most favourable grace; and supplicating an answer,

I remain your obedient and anxious servant.

P.S. Pray do not pay the postage of your letter. I shall esteem it as a touching earnest of your friendship, if you will allow me to pay the twopence.

Gradually the Governesses' Benevolent Institution was able to offer constructive help to the governess and the scope of its work was broadened. The first mention of an examination for governesses was in 1844, when David Laing corresponded with the National Society[1] and the Archbishop of Canterbury, because the committee felt that certificates of qualification as the result of an examination would raise both the status and the standards of governesses. For the next two years the plan was held in

[3] The National Society for promoting the education of the poor in the principles of the Established Church.

abeyance, while the committee concentrated its attention on the purchase of a house, where governesses might stay for short periods while they looked for a new position. 66 Harley Street (when the houses were re-numbered, this became number 47) was purchased for £1700, and not only did it become 'The Home' for numerous governesses, but it was also the office where governesses and prospective employers might register their names, to the advantage of both parties. A committee of ladies was formed to help to run the house, and it became a busy centre. The existence of a registry made an assessment of an applicant's capabilities even more desirable. A good testimonial might mean only that a governess could keep her charges quiet and out of the way of their parents, and no more. Yet another plan was set on foot for an Asylum for aged governesses, and this was opened in Kentish Town in 1848.

The Honourable Amelia Murray, a maid of honour to Queen Victoria, was quite independently another firm supporter of the governesses' cause. During a long life she supported many philanthropic schemes; she was also a person of some spirit, for in 1856 she resigned her position in the Queen's bedchamber after a visit to the United States, so that she could be free to advocate the abolition of slavery. During the 1840s she was much concerned with educational schemes. In a letter addressed to the G.B.I. in 1847, she referred to her 'frequent communication' with a Dr Wilson, concerning the possible co-operation of the College of Preceptors[1] in a plan for 'aiding and elevating' governesses. Her plans, however, were either thwarted or postponed, and the money she had given for the purpose was given to the G.B.I. It is assumed that her influence was instrumental in securing Queen Victoria's support of the Institution, and later of Queen's College. It is of interest that in 1847 Amelia Murray published a book entitled *Remarks on Education*, in which she expressed ideas which had much in common with those of Maurice. She

[1] Founded in 1846. It adopted many of the functions performed by the G.B.I., including the establishment of a register of teachers. Women were admitted in 1849. See *The College of Preceptors: fifty years of progress in education* (1896).

disapproved of corporal punishment in any school, and she disliked competition: 'let us banish emulation as the leading motive, and promote love and good will'.

By the spring of 1847, David Laing was in close communication with several interested parties, including some of the staff of King's College, about both lectures and examinations for governesses. In April 1847, he received a letter from Adolphus Bernays, the Professor of German Literature at King's College. The letter began thus:

> The perusal of Miss Maurice's[1] admirable book, *Mothers and Governesses* and the statements I heard at the late dinner, have interested me in favour of the Governesses Benevolent Institution, that I wish to do something for its benefit. Now as to the small share of the world's gold and silver that I am enabled to earn by my professional labours, I have so many calls for it that I could spare but little. But I may manage to give you a little of my time which, if successfully applied, may produce a decent sum. I propose therefore to give at the Governesses' Home a course of instruction in the German language in twenty lessons of two hours each, half in autumn before Christmas, and half immediately after that festival, the proceeds, after deducting the expense for advertisements, to go towards the fund for the Asylum. I have selected this branch of your admirable institution, because it seems to me to be as much wanted as any of the others and yet to be the least advanced.
>
> I should propose that the instruction should be confined to ladies, and to boys under 13 years of age accompanied by a female relation; that there should be one lesson a week, on an afternoon between 2 and 4; that the terms should be for half the course two guineas, and for the whole three guineas, governesses at the Home to be admitted either gratuitously or at half the fee . . .[2]

[1] Mary Maurice, sister of F. D. Maurice.
[2] Governesses' Papers I, pp. 359–62.

Another letter came from Tom Taylor, a Professor at University College and later the editor of *Punch*:

> If you think I can be of any service, in connection with the subject of English, to the Educational department of the Governesses' Benevolent Institution, I shall be glad to aid you in any way you may determine on, at all consistent with my other engagements. The Ladies declined my offer in terms so diplomatic that I could not precisely understand them. But as I made it in real sympathy with the society in its main objects, I should be acting inconsistently in allowing their answer to stand in the way of my acceptance of your invitation. I have, at all events, the distinction of dealing with a subject very little understood, tho' very generally professed to be taught, even by governesses who profess little else.
>
> I need not say that any assistance, if required, will be given gratuitously to the society—or that any fees resulting from lectures, should lectures be given, will be at the service of the directors of your institution.[1]

There were other offers of help too, and some lectures were held at the Home during the summer and autumn of 1847.

By this time, the committee of the G.B.I. had decided that they wanted to pursue the idea of issuing a qualification for governesses, with or without the active support of the Government. At the committee meeting in June, David Laing reported that the Government had 'professed themselves not unfriendly to the idea, but were unwilling to commit themselves to any new measure'. Laing had begun to fear 'that delay might throw the work into other hands, by whom it would be imperfectly undertaken and badly done'. He had therefore 'ventured to apply for the use of Her Majesty's name, which had been most readily and graciously accorded'. All this was approved by the committee, who then agreed to invite nine lecturers or professors connected with King's to give lectures to the governesses. They realised

[1] Governesses' Papers II, pp. 93–4.

more and more clearly that it was quite unsatisfactory to award certificates without providing education as well.

The nine professors met together the following month to discuss the plan further with David Laing. They formed themselves into a Committee of Education, and decided that they must acquire some more premises as soon as possible. In September, the G.B.I. bought the lease of 67 Harley Street, next door to the Home.

The Committee of Education held its first formal meeting on October 13 1847, in the Marsden Library of King's College. From that time, it may be said that Queen's College was launched.

That this first college for women should have been the concern of Frederick Denison Maurice and his friends and associates from King's College was its greatest good fortune. Maurice was one of the great Christian thinkers and teachers of the nineteenth century, though it is only in the twentieth century that his teaching and achievements are being fully appreciated. It is time for us to look at his personality and his motives and ideas in carrying out this scheme.

II

F. D. Maurice

ANYONE who remembers what it is like to sit and listen to a lesson or a lecture will appreciate the compliment paid to the founder of Queen's by one of its early students, Camilla Croudace:

> There was no fidgeting during Mr Maurice's lecture, no looking at the clock, or shutting up of inkstands with a snap when the hour came for the lecture to finish.

All who met or listened to this small, gentle man, came away impressed by his quiet depth, his humility and his sincerity.

His influence was in no way ephemeral. It is remarkable that the two educational enterprises with which he was closely associated, Queen's and the Working Men's College, have retained their original character to this day; that while some of his educational ideas appear irrelevant to the twentieth century, others are only just being recognised; and that as a thinker and theologian he is attracting more attention now than in his own day.

The portraits of him reveal a sensitive, sometimes sad man. The experiences of his life left their scars, though they never shook his faith. He came to know sorrow young; as he grew up he met it frequently, and it was an ever-deepening experience. By 1848, he had lost three of his sisters, one of his greatest friends, and now most recently, his wife; and he was only forty-three.

John Frederick Denison Maurice was the only surviving boy in a family of eight children. He was born in 1805: this made him a year younger than Disraeli and four years older than Gladstone. He came in the middle of the family, and grew up with his seven sisters, first in Normanstone, near Yarmouth and then in Frenchay, near Bristol. His father, Michael Maurice, was a Unitarian minister who took in resident pupils; this meant that there were boys for Maurice to play with, though he remained close to several of his sisters throughout their lives. Until he was ten, he was educated with two of his younger sisters, Emma and Priscilla, by a governess to the family named Esther Parker. At the age of ten, he was taken into his father's group of pupils and educated with them until he left to stay with cousins with the intention of reading for the Bar, a course which he abandoned for Cambridge in 1823.

Maurice's father had been brought up in the theological tradition of the English Presbyterians, who had abandoned trinitarian belief in the eighteenth century, and throughout his life he clung to his liberal unitarian belief. Maurice's mother and sisters, on the other hand, changed to more orthodox views. The event which precipitated this change was the death of Edmund Hurry, a cousin of the Maurice children who lived with them. It was the first experience of sorrow for the family and they felt it deeply. It prompted a crisis for the family and for each individual separately, and it led all but the father to adopt a more orthodox Christian standpoint.

Each member of the family had inherently, and was encouraged by circumstance to develop, a highly individual outlook. The household was the scene of tense religious division, which the father felt deeply. At one time husband and wife could only discuss religious matters by letter—it was too painful a topic for conversation. The elder sisters were forbidden to talk to the young Maurice about religion. No wonder that he later wrote that 'these years were to me years of moral confusion and contradiction'. The effect of this background was to show, first, in Maurice's own originality of thought—he felt compelled to think out his own theological position and to remain loyal to these convictions once established—and secondly, he grew up with a deep desire for the unity of all Christians and a profound dislike for religious controversy. He would attach himself to no religious party in the Church of England (which he joined as a young man) and disliked all theological systems. He wrote:

> The desire for *Unity* has haunted me all my life through; I have never been able to substitute any desire for that, or to

> accept any of the different schemes for satisfying it which men have devised.[1]

Twenty years before Queen's opened, he was not only writing on the deficiencies of existing education for girls, in a Cambridge magazine which he and some of his friends had started; he was also teaching his sisters. He spent one long vacation teaching his three youngest sisters. Lucilla later wrote:

> He began Greek with us on a plan of his own making us form our own grammar and reading at once in the Iliad and the New Testament.[2]

The same method of teaching is described much later by one of his Queen's pupils:

> In the papers we had to write for him, anything like borrowed opinions, second-hand criticisms of books which one had not read, was in his eyes a breach of honesty, and he knew how to make one feel desperately ashamed of it. On the other hand, there never was anyone so kind and encouraging to even the most halting attempts at thinking for one's self, and writing one's own thoughts.[3]

Of his teachers at Cambridge, the one who influenced him most was Julius Hare. Maurice later wrote that

> to his [Hare's] Lectures on Sophocles and Plato I can trace the most permanent effect on my character, and on all my modes of contemplating subjects, natural, human and divine.[4]

Hare for his part regarded Maurice as one of the ablest pupils he

[1] From 'an incomplete autobiographical attempt', quoted in J. F. Maurice, *Life of F. D. Maurice* (1884), vol. I, p. 41.
[2] *Family Records* by Lucilla Powell, MS.
[3] Queen's College Magazine, 1891, pp. 76–7.
[4] J. F. Maurice, *Life of F. D. Maurice* (1884), vol. I, p. 55.

had encountered, but found him almost impossibly shy. This shyness and reserve stayed with him all his life, and his friends felt they never really understood him. There was a certain aloofness and isolation about him which distinguishes some other great Christian thinkers.

Also at Cambridge, Maurice joined the select and active Cambridge Conversazione Society, nicknamed 'The Apostles'. The members met every Saturday evening to hear and discuss an essay by one of the members. These debates really provided the effective university education of the undergraduates who attended. Maurice's friends there included John Sterling, Richard Trench, Arthur Hallam and Tennyson. These friendships were longlasting and influential, and it was from this circle that many of the first supporters of Queen's were to come.

As well as talking and debating with the Apostles, Maurice and another friend, Whitmore, began a magazine in Cambridge, *The Metropolitan Quarterly Magazine*. The first issue was published in November 1825, to be followed by only two more issues. What concerns us here is that Maurice contributed an unusually interesting and perceptive article on Female Education,[1] exposing the 'mean and insignificant' studies and the 'trivial pursuits' which passed for education in most establishments of female learning:

> What is chiefly remarkable in the first division of female education is, the great tenderness which is observed towards the pupil whenever any exertion is required of her intellect, and the corresponding hard measure which is dealt out to her when any exactions are to be laid on the memory. School-mistresses and governantes are very clever reasoners from analogy, and they wisely conclude that, as in the case of the senses, the extinction of one is always accompanied by a great increase of vigour and acuteness in the rest; so with regard to the faculties of the mind, it is only necessary that one should be depressed to the lowest point of imbecility, in order that those which remain may acquire an almost unlimited capacity of exertion. Having

[1] *Metropolitan Quarterly Magazine*, II, pp. 265–82.

> settled this point in their minds, they could have no difficulty in determining which particular faculty should be slaughtered for the sake of its brethren. The intellect is proud, obstinate, and uncompromising, fond of power, and not willing to succumb even to the easy yoke of lady mothers and lady governesses. The memory, on the contrary, is good tempered and docile, has no opinion or will of its own, receives instructions submissively, and obeys them as far as it is able. To the great task, therefore, of giving a proper and rightful superiority to this exemplary faculty have these ladies addressed themselves.

The usual material for study was to be found in catechisms and inferior books.

> the books which are put into young ladies' hands are amongst the worst that have been written upon every subject; but to make up for this deficiency, they have to learn them by heart.

The one faculty which was abhorred above all was the imagination.

> the imagination . . . is a terrible object of the dread, the hatred, and hostility of the mistress of establishments, and the governess of young ladies . . . We believe it will be generally found necessary to eradicate the imagination before any decisive attempt is made to encourage that fondness for trivial pursuits, the inculcation of which forms so capital an article in the institution of every Christian woman.

Instead of this travesty of education, he says, girls are in a position to enjoy true learning, for 'it is the happiest incident in the condition of women, that they are exempt from the necessity of being prepared for professional avocations'. Above all, men prefer a person who has 'thought more deeply than she has read, and felt more deeply than she has thought'.

What could Maurice have known at this time about girls' education? He had three elder sisters and four younger. For a time they had a governess, who taught Maurice as well as his younger sisters. None of his sisters was a typical product of the kind of education he describes, and none had her imagination or her intellect stunted. We have already remarked on the high degree of originality which each one showed. But this was perhaps in spite of the education they received, and not because of it.

Maurice left Cambridge in 1826, without a degree. He gained a first in the Civil Law examinations; but in order to take the degree, he was required also to declare himself a member of the Church of England. Though he was now moving nearer to membership of that church, he had not yet made up his mind, and he refused to commit himself; in turning his back on a degree, he was, as his father wrote to a friend, preserving his principles at the expense of his interest, for he was reasonably certain to have been offered a fellowship. This was the integrity which illuminated his life to the end.

After Cambridge, Maurice came to London and spent three years studying law and writing for various journals. In his contributions to *The Westminster Review* and *The Athenaeum*, Maurice made frequent reference to his views on education, including his admiration for Pestalozzi. He and his friend Sterling joined the London Debating Society, a society formed originally by supporters of Robert Owen, but later open to opponents of Owenism; this proved a forum for lively debate. Amongst the members were John Stuart Mill, Macaulay and Samuel Wilberforce. Mill writes in his *Autobiography* that

> almost every debate was a *bataille rangée* between the 'philosophic Radicals' and the Tory lawyers; until our conflicts were talked about, and several persons of note and consideration came to hear us. This happened still more in the subsequent season, 1828 and 1829, when the Coleridgians, in the persons of Maurice and Sterling, made their appearance in the society as a second Liberal and even Radical party, on totally different grounds from Benthamism and

> vehemently opposed to it; bringing into these discussions the general doctrines and modes of thought of the European reaction against the philosophy of the eighteenth century; and adding a third and very important belligerent party to our contests, which were now no bad exponent of the movement of opinion among the most cultivated part of the new generation.[1]

From the time when he first went up to Cambridge, Maurice came under the influence of Coleridge and Carlyle. He 'came nearer to treating Coleridge as a master than he did anyone else'.[2]

It was at this time that Maurice had the opportunity to learn more about the teaching of children at first hand. In 1828, Michael Maurice, his father, lost a great deal of his money—much of it was invested in the bonds of the constitutional party in Spain. The grown-up children of the family felt obliged to earn their livings. Elizabeth, the eldest, became a companion to Gladstone's sister; Mary opened a school in the family home (now removed to Southampton) and Priscilla took a teaching post in Brixton.

Mary was the most enterprising. She decided to take as her model the school recently established by Dr Mayo at Cheam and went to stay with his sister, Elizabeth Mayo, to study the school at first hand. Dr Mayo was the most celebrated English disciple of Pestalozzi and his school had already established a considerable reputation.[3] No doubt Mary Maurice discussed what she had seen and what she thought about it with her brother. She was probably responsible for introducing him to the G.B.I. in the first place, and she later helped him at Queen's.

Meanwhile Maurice had returned to university study in Oxford. There he read Theology, was baptised into the Church of England and ordained to its ministry two years later. An important stage in his spiritual pilgrimage was completed. He had a

[1] J. S. Mill, *Autobiography* (1873), p. 128.
[2] See Alec Vidler, *F. D. Maurice and Company* (1966), ch. 9.
[3] See Kate Silber, *Pestalozzi* (1960), Appendix I, Pestalozzianism in Britain and the United States.

short spell as a curate in Warwickshire and then came to London as Chaplain at Guy's Hospital. Here he found satisfaction in combining pastoral work among the great variety of patients there with continued academic study.

In 1838 he married Anna Barton, and during the seven years of their married life both were exceedingly happy. It was also a productive period in Maurice's life. In 1838 he published the book which is generally regarded as his finest, *The Kingdom of Christ*, with the sub-title *Hints to a Quaker respecting the principles, constitution and ordinances of the Catholic Church. The Kingdom of Christ* was a work of theology, prompted by a dispute among the Society of Friends. Thinking and writing about this dispute 'led him to articulate profound and seminal thoughts about the Being of God and the status of mankind in the universe, about the nature of the Catholic Church and its most familiar institutions, about both civil and ecclesiastical polity and the relations of Church and State'.[1] He described himself to one of his friends, Ludlow, as 'only a digger'; this was one of his great virtues—in order to penetrate deeply into every problem he dug down to its basic principles. This is why his works are still read today.

Maurice was a theologian and a deep thinker. But he was equally concerned with the practical application of theology, to the social and political problems of the community. 'No man, I think,' he wrote (in a much-quoted phrase from a letter he wrote to Derwent Coleridge), 'will ever be of much use to his generation, who does not apply himself mainly to the questions which are occupying those who belong to it.' No other clergyman of the nineteenth century was more immersed in the practical life of the community, while simultaneously so prodigal with his pen. The only person to approach Maurice's combination of theology with social involvement was Charles Kingsley, who was associated with Maurice in the Queen's project as in others.

In 1839 Maurice gave a series of lectures, later published with the title *Has the Church, or the State, the Power to Educate the*

[1] F. D. Maurice, *The Kingdom of Christ* (S. C. M. 1958), Introduction by Alec Vidler, p. 7.

Nation? The occasion of the lectures was the increase in the grant given by the central government to the two school societies[1] from £20,000 a year to £30,000, a proposal which had generated a vigorous discussion on the merits of an inspection of grant-aided schools, and on the role of the churches in providing education—a burning issue in nineteenth-century politics. Maurice prepared his lectures in a hurry, having issued the tickets before preparing his notes. These lectures are not easy to read today. In their acceptance of class divisions and insistence on the church's control of education, we must regard them as out-of-date. But in their emphasis on co-operation rather than on competition, and in their distrust of education which emphasises provable facts at the expense of opinion and understanding, we must regard them as enlightened and far-seeing.

Maurice's intellectual reputation was well established before 1848. In 1836 he had refused an invitation to become a tutor at Downing College, Cambridge; a month later he was nominated for the Professorship of Political Economy at Oxford, but then withdrew his name. In 1840, after some years as Chaplain at Guy's Hospital, he was elected as Professor of English Literature and Modern History at King's College, London. Six years later, he was elected as Professor of Divinity, and Chaplain of Lincoln's Inn. In 1843, he was pressed to allow his name to be put forward as the new Principal of King's. He refused. 'If ever I am to do anything for the Church it must be in some subordinate position,' he wrote to Julius Hare.

He had already published several books, and was involved in more than one theological controversy. It must be admitted that his arguments are not always easy to understand, and that the present-day reader must grapple with them before they will yield their meaning. He was too much a scholar and original thinker to be content with generalisations and conventional statements. Many of his students at King's who were not prepared to make much effort found him too difficult to understand, for he made

[1] The National Society for promoting the education of the poor in the principles of the Established Church (founded 1811), and The British and Foreign School Society (founded 1814).

few concessions to them. Canon Farrar[1] later wrote, 'I never in my life attended any history lectures which dealt so little with facts.' The more able and perceptive students, however, recognised a person and an intellect of distinction.

There is one other sphere of his work to be mentioned before we turn to his work at Queen's; his association with the Christian Socialist movement. Never an academic recluse, he became increasingly preoccupied with the 'condition of England' question in the 1840s, and with the attempts of reformers to create a satisfying way of life in a society which was rapidly becoming industrialised and urbanised. In England, the Chartists, working-class men who were denied any share in the government of the country, had already made two attempts to present their Charter to Parliament, and in Paris, Socialist ideas were gaining currency. In 1843, Maurice was corresponding with Daniel Macmillan about providing simple articles for the working classes. By the middle of 1848 he was committed to the working-class cause. He summed up his aim in a letter to his friend Ludlow: 'our great desire is to Christianise Socialism,' for 'Christian Socialism is in my mind the assertion of God's order'.

Thus Maurice in the year of the foundation of Queen's College was a man of considerable intellectual stature, fully involved in both the philosophical and political problems of his age, and ready to give his loyalty and service generously to any cause in which he believed.

[1] Canon F. W. Farrar, author of *Eric, or Little by Little* and other books.

III

The College — Planning

ALMOST all the members of the Committee of Education formed in the autumn of 1847 were members of the staff of King's College in the Strand. King's College was then twenty years old. It had been founded by supporters of the Church of England in reply to the unsectarian University College (called the University of London, but initially without a charter) in Gower Street. There were no religious tests for admission to King's, but the professors (unless they taught modern or oriental languages) were required to be communicant members of the Church of England, and the atmosphere was orthodox Anglican. The object of the College was to prepare young men of sixteen and over, either for a career in commerce, or for further academic education at Oxford or Cambridge—an equivalent of the modern college of further education or sixth form college. The education given was general rather than specialist, until the Theological Department was added to the college in 1846; this provided a two-year course leading to ordination, for graduates and others who were recommended. The college established its reputation chiefly by the academic successes of its former students at Oxford and Cambridge, successes which were considerable.

When Maurice was Professor of English Literature and Modern History, he was required to give only two lectures a week, one on each subject. His colleagues, many of them also clergymen, also spent just two or three hours giving lectures at King's, and so had time available to help with this new project of giving lectures to governesses.

One of these colleagues played a prominent part in planning the new college, and was even referred to by some people (including himself) as a co-founder. If one takes into account the amount of time he spent on planning, teaching and administration, this claim might be justified. But he left no permanent imprint on the college, and was not a popular colleague among the staff, though appreciated as a teacher by his students. He was Charles Grenfell Nicolay, the Librarian at King's.

Nicolay's own formal education was marginal, but he devoted himself enthusiastically to numerous educational ventures during a long life. He was the seventh of eight children of a widowed mother, and was virtually left to educate himself. His later reputation and his published writings on geography show that he was a keen and meticulous scholar. For example, he published *The Principles of Physical Geography* as a textbook for Eton College; he published a book on *The Oregon Territory*; and he lectured four times to the British Association. In spite of this, he suffered from feelings of inferiority because of his lack of university education; as a result he was overbearing, opinionated and difficult to get on with. Tactlessness was his undoing on more than one occasion.

He was ordained to a curacy in the Scilly Isles in 1841, and came to King's as Librarian in 1843, combining this position with the Chaplaincy of King's College Hospital, and later, a Lectureship in Geography at King's.

In London, Nicolay met at least two of the enterprising women who wanted to gather help in providing some formal education for girls. He was 'a proposed officer' in the college for which Amelia Murray was collecting money in 1844, and it was on his own suggestion that he threw in his lot with the G.B.I. when Amelia Murray abandoned her own scheme. Julia Smith was another acquaintance; she was not directly connected with Queen's, but she was a friend and supporter of Mrs Reid, the founder of Bedford College.

This is how Nicolay described the foundation of Queen's, writing nearly forty years later, when he was settled in Australia:

> . . . I should acknowledge that the College originated in a want, felt no doubt by many, but expressed to me by two ladies who had long been engaged in tuition, the one as an aunt, the other as a governess, and that my connection with King's College enabled me to supply that want by the establishment of Queen's College, and by the numerous similar institutions which, following the example set by it,

> were founded in most of the large towns in Great Britain. It may interest your readers to know that the aunt was Miss Julia Smith, aunt of Florence Nightingale . . .[1]

Plans for the college were being made throughout the summer of 1847 by the G.B.I. committee. Much correspondence passed between Nicolay and David Laing, Nicolay concerning himself very much with administrative details. Laing wrote to Nicolay in June:

> It was my wish that Mr Maurice should take Theology, be principal, or chairman of examiners, and be responsible for the lecturers.

But Maurice would not agree to take the position of Principal. He wrote to Laing in the same month:

> I should very much object to undertake the office of Principal, as it could set me above my present colleagues at King's College. Jelf (Principal of King's) has no objections to my giving theological lectures if I have the Bishop's sanction which I think we should seek and might obtain for the College generally. It seems to me that the Principal ought not to be a widower or bachelor and that his wife should have experience in Education and be competent to exercise some control over pupils in the College. But upon this I am not certain. I think it is very desirable that the whole arrangement of the Institution should be very carefully considered before it is launched especially as it is to bear the Queen's name and must, as a first attempt, have great influence upon all that should arise hereafter as a model or a warning.[1]

Maurice refused to change his mind, and served as Chairman of the Committee of Education; there was no Principal until 1855, when the Chairman of the Committee of Education was

[1] *Perth Inquirer and Commercial News,* January 5 1883.
[2] Governesses' Papers I, pp. 373–4.

1 Frederick Denison Maurice, Founder of the College
Drawing by Samuel Laurence

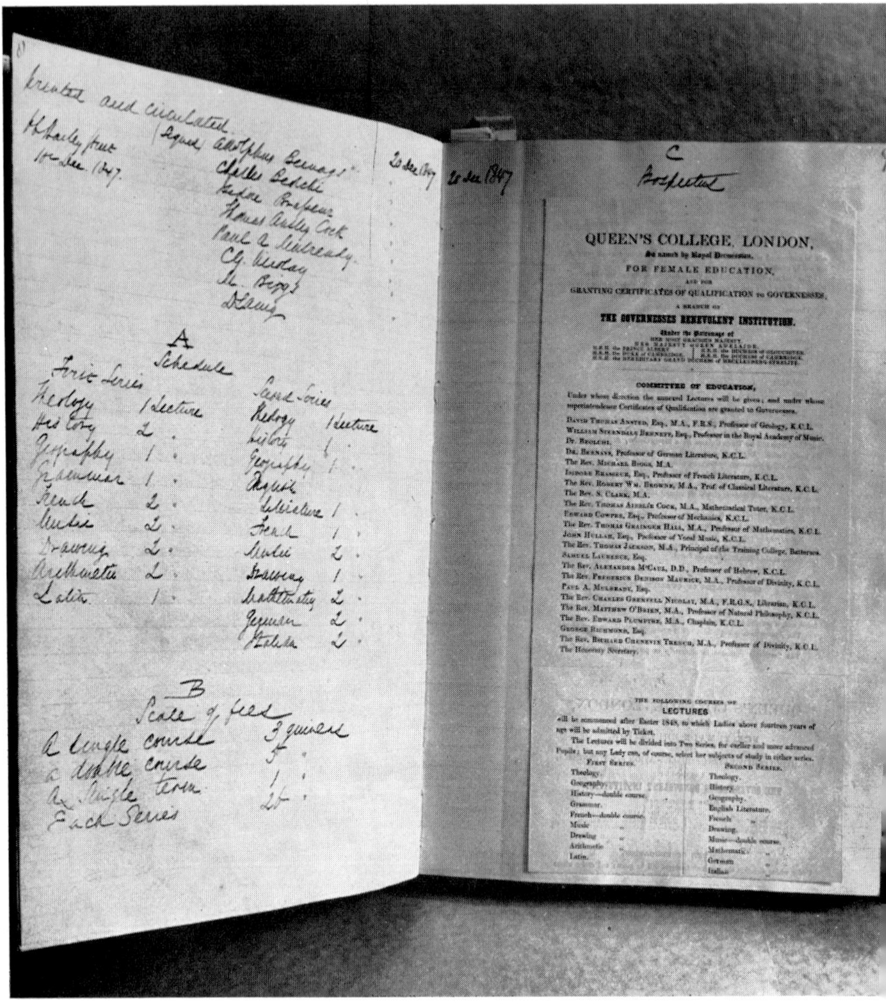

2 Early pages of the first minute book of the Committee of Education of Queen's College

also given the title of Principal, and the Deputy Chairman the title of Dean.

The Committee of Education appointed by the G.B.I. committee had its first official meeting on October 13 at King's, and began to plan the curriculum. It consisted of members of the staff of King's College, and David Laing as secretary. They arranged for the granting of certificates to begin in December, and for the formal programme of lectures in the following May.

It is difficult now to realise what a pioneer project they were undertaking. There were in 1848 no opportunities for women to share formally in the advantages of higher education, though really determined individuals educated themselves by reading and conversation in intellectual company. Dominating the contemporary writings on the position of women in society was a strong moral and ethical tone, reminding the reader that her religion bade her accept the condition in which she found herself. 'The first thing of importance is to be content to be inferior to men—inferior in mental power in the proportion that you are inferior in bodily strength.'[1]

Yet women were charged with the task of educating children, either as mothers, elementary schoolmistresses or governesses. No thought was given to adequate preparation for the task, and most people were content to ignore the abysmal standards of instruction, as they ignored many other unpleasant aspects of life in early Victorian England. In 1842, Whitelands College was founded as the first women's training college; eight more followed in the next four years. The standard required for entrance at Whitelands indicates the general expectation of attainment. The candidate was required to produce a testimonial from the clergyman of her parish, to prove that she was able 'to read fluently and with intelligence, to write correctly from dictation, and to work the first four rules of arithmetic with readiness and precision', and to show 'a certain degree of acquaintance with the history and doctrine of the Holy Scriptures'.[2]

[1] Mrs William Ellis, *Daughters of England* (1843), pp. 11–12.
[2] See R. W. Rich, *The training of teachers in England and Wales during the nineteenth century* (1933).

The universities of Oxford and Cambridge were closed to women until the later part of the nineteenth century. Bedford College[1] in London is the oldest university college for women. It was founded in 1849, a matter of months after Queen's first opened its doors to students. We shall consider its relation to Queen's in a later chapter. Here we need note only two things; first, that it is almost, but not quite, as old as Queen's, and that if its foundation was already being discussed, the discussions were confined to a drawing-room on the edge of Regent's Park; and secondly, that it began, as did Queen's, for 'ladies' over the age of twelve, so that neither institution could set its standards too high.

Of the two university colleges in London, University College[2] was the first to admit women students. In 1828, Antonio Panizzi, then Professor of Italian, asked the College authorities for permission to hold his lectures on Italian life in a place where ladies might be admitted; the lectures were duly given in Willis' Rooms, King Street, and ladies formed a large part of the audience. This was as much an effort to find more students as an excess of zeal for the education of women on Panizzi's part; he was feeling frustrated with only about five students of Italian in the College itself. In 1832 two women registered at the College to attend a juvenile course on Natural Philosophy, but there was no further female registration until 1861.

The other college, King's, first attracted women to the lectures given by Charles Lyell in the summer of 1832. The subject was Geology; the main thesis was that the creation story in Genesis could not be taken literally. The lectures were of magnetic attraction, and the wives and daughters of the professors flocked into the College to hear them. The Council of King's was alarmed, and hurriedly passed a resolution

> that the attendance of ladies be not permitted at any course of lectures to be hereafter read in the college, and

[1] See Margaret Tuke, *A history of Bedford College for women 1849–1937*. (1939).

[2] See H. Hale Bellot, *University College, London, 1826–1926*. (1929).

> that the several professors be made acquainted with this regulation.[1]

When the wives, daughters and friends tried to attend Wheatstone's lectures on electricity in 1848, the ban was reiterated. But in 1878 the staff delivered a series of lectures to ladies in Kensington, leading to the establishment of a separate women's department. Women were first admitted to the actual premises at King's for Saturday morning and weekday evening lectures in 1880, but only after long and serious debate. One other educational institution, the London Mechanics' Institute (later Birkbeck College) admitted women in 1830 to its lectures, but three years later was still considering 'the propriety of admitting females attending lectures through the front entrance.'[2]

There were some opportunities for attending lectures and using libraries. Dorothea Beale, later a student and tutor at Queen's, and famous as headmistress of Cheltenham Ladies' College, spent three years at home between attending a boarding school and a finishing school in Paris, and attended lectures at the Literary Society at Crosby Hall, of which her father was secretary. She and her sisters used Crosby Hall library. In her autobiography,[3] she wrote that 'the works of Froissart, Thierry, Thiers, Alison, Miller's *Philosophy of History*, Sir James Stephen's books, Prescott's, Creasy's, stand out very distinctly to memory'. A few women were finding their way to the mecca of scholars—the Reading Room of the British Museum. A writer on London had this to say about 'the fair visitants of the Reading Room':

> They are not numerous, but they are ominous of a social revolution . . . It is beyond question that the habit of seeing ladies publicly engaged in literary pursuits is familiarising the minds of a portion of society to the coming revolution,

[1] See F. J. C. Hearnshaw, *The Centenary History of King's College* (1929).
[2] See C. D. Burns, *Short History of Birkbeck College* (1924).
[3] See Elizabeth Raikes, *Dorothea Beale of Cheltenham* (1908), which has quotations from Dorothea Beale's manuscript autobiography.

> as the independent habit of thought and action, produced in them by a remunerative profession, is bringing it about.[1]

From the biographies and autobiographies of pioneers of women's education in the nineteenth century (as well as from novels), one finds time and again accounts of the well-meaning but unenlightened forms of teaching in girls' schools. Dorothea Beale considered that her school was well above the average, and yet

> history was learned by committing to memory little manuals; rules of arithmetic were taught, but the principles were never explained. Instead of reading and learning the masterpieces of literature, we repeated week by week the Lamentation of Hezekiah, the pretty but somewhat weak *Mother's Picture* of Cowper, and worse doggerel verses on the solar system.[2]

Anna Swanwick, one of the most intelligent women of her generation, had a similar experience:

> In my young days, though I attended what was considered the best girls' school in Liverpool, the education there given was so meagre that I felt like the Peri excluded from Paradise, and I often longed to assume the costume of a boy in order to learn Latin, Greek and Mathematics, which were then regarded as essential to a liberal education for boys, but were not thought of for girls . . . during my school-days I never remember to have seen a map, while all my knowledge of geography was derived from passages learnt by rote. The teaching of grammar and of other subjects was on a par with that of geography.[3]

[1] Charles Knight, *London*, vol. IV (1843), Ch. C.
[2] Quoted from MS. Autobiography in E. Raikes, *Dorothea Beale of Cheltenham* (1908).
[3] Quoted in M. L. Bruce, *Anna Swanwick* (1903).

When Dorothea Beale went to teach in the Clergy Daughters' School at Casterton, she found she was expected to teach, to girls of sixteen and seventeen, scripture, arithmetic, mathematics, ancient, modern and church history, geography, English, French, German, Latin and Italian. On the whole, as she remarked, the less a teacher knew, the more ambitious was she in her range of subjects. Such education could only be of the most superficial kind. There were exceptions, but the majority of governesses lacked the elementary skills of spelling and correct grammar. They rarely aimed higher than the purveyance of ill-understood facts.

There were women of culture and learning, from whom in so many cases, the early pioneers of female education came. They were the products of cultured and educated homes. Here one has to quote from Dorothea Beale's family again. Her aunt Elizabeth Complin, who helped Dorothea with her education, understood Latin, Greek and Hebrew, and liked reading philosophy. Her great-aunt, Mrs Cornwallis, had learnt Hebrew and had written several books. Mrs Cornwallis' daughter, Caroline, studied Greek, Latin and Hebrew, and wrote prolifically, not only for *The Westminster Review* and *Fraser's Magazine*, but also a series of *Small Books on Great Subjects*. Dorothea's father, Miles Beale, a surgeon, made his home in London a meeting place for literary and artistic people. He liked reading to his children and discussing with them the books they had read.

Even for Dorothea Beale, there was no opportunity for systematic study. She tried to teach herself geometry and worked through the first six books of Euclid, but did not really grasp the subject properly until she was taught by Professor Cock at Queen's.

It was against this background that the Committee of Education had to decide what sort of education to provide at the new college. The subjects were decided on in January 1848, and the lecturers chosen. It was agreed that there should be an introductory lecture in each subject during the first week of the term after Easter, and after that a regular series of lectures, with a professor assigned to each subject. This is the list to which they agreed:

Arithmetic:	Rev Thomas Astley Cock, classes
Drawing:	George Richmond or Samuel Laurence, an introductory lecture Paul Mulready, classes
English Literature:	Rev F. D. Maurice or Tom Taylor, introductory lecture Rev C. G. Nicolay, lectures
French:	Professor Isidore Brasseur, classes
German:	Professor Bernays, classes
English Grammar:	Tom Taylor
Latin:	Tom Taylor
Geography:	Tom Taylor or Rev F. D. Maurice, introductory lecture
History:	Rev C. G. Nicolay, classes
Mathematics:	Rev T. G. Hall, introductory lecture Rev T. A. Cock, classes
Theology:	Rev R. C. Trench, introductory lecture Rev Michael Biggs, classes
Italian:	Dr Charles Beolchi, classes
Mechanics:	Professor Cowper
Method in teaching:	Rev Thomas Jackson
Physical Geography and Geology:	Professor Ansted

We will reserve comment on the subjects and the lecturers for a later chapter, since the professors and subjects were in some cases changed.

At first, it was decided that the lectures were to be open to all ladies over fourteen, but the age was reduced to twelve before the College actually opened. At its fourth meeting, the committee decided that the lectures would not be confined to governesses or intending governesses, but would be open to any young ladies who wished to come.

This was a most important decision. The education to be given at Queen's, then as now, was not to be in any sense narrowly vocational. This point was dealt with by Maurice in his Inaugural

Lecture.[1] He gave three reasons why the Committee had decided not to confine themselves to educating actual or aspiring governesses. The first was that 'those who had no dream of entering upon such a work this year, might be forced by some reverse of fortune to think of it next year'. The second, that almost every woman finds herself a teacher at some time of her life, either of her own children, or her younger sisters, or other people's children. And the third and most important, that 'though the mere art of teaching is no doubt worthy of diligent study, and should form a part in all sound education, still the main qualification of a governess is not an acquaintance with this method or that, but a real grounded knowledge of that which is to be taught, and a sympathy with those who are to learn from her'.

It was agreed that 'any young lady may select such particular classes as will meet her own views'—a tradition which has continued to the present day with the provision for both compounders and non-compounders, compounders taking a full-time course, and non-compounders taking only a few classes weekly. The fees were to be either nine guineas a term for attendance at any number of classes, or a guinea and a half per term for a subject with two classes a week.

One other provision had to be made. It was unthinkable in 1848 that young ladies should attend a lecture given by a male professor without being chaperoned. A scheme was therefore drawn up for a body of Lady Visitors who would attend the lectures on a rota basis, and would be invited to 'make suggestions in a locked book kept for that purpose'—a book which is still in the College's possession. The unfortunate weakness of the scheme was the lack of communication between the Lady Visitors and the all-male Committee of Education, which led to strong feelings on both sides, and one or two serious crises, in the first decade of the College's life. Also, the Lady Visitors varied in their devotion to duty. To some it was purely part of the social round. As Thackeray observed, the London woman had to find time 'to call

[1] Published in *The First College for Women*, ed. Mrs A. Tweedie (1898) and in *Introductory Lectures delivered at Queen's College* (1849).

upon ladies of her own station, either domestically or in her public character in which she sits upon Charity Committees or Ball Committees or Emigration Committees, or Queen's College Committees, and discharges I don't know what more duties of British stateswomanship'.[1] Others took their responsibilities more seriously. Altogether the Lady Visitors proved an active, vociferous and influential group of ladies whom the Committee of Education ignored at their peril.

Maurice, we have already stated, was to be Chairman of the Committee, and Nicolay was appointed deputy chairman. Nicolay's was the more time-consuming task, for he was charged with responsibility as 'the organ of communication' between the Committee of Education, the examiners for governesses' certificates, the Lady Visitors, the Lady Resident, the pupils and the servants, and with the arrangement of lecture rooms and meetings. Though industrious and enthusiastic for the cause, Nicolay did not have the personality or tact for this position. A Lady Resident was to receive the pupils when they arrived, and to be responsible for domestic arrangements.

The examinations for certificates began on December 23 1847. There appears at the head of the certificates for the first time, 'Queen's College, London'. But since Queen's was primarily an educating rather than an examining institution, it is appropriate to consider May 1 1848, the date when the first students arrived for the first lectures, as the official opening date of the college.

The first ladies who successfully presented themselves for examination were Isabella Merritt and Matilda Mary Wallis Oxley, both in Italian. The first certificate, copied into a register, reads as follows:

> Miss Isabella Merritt having offered herself for Examination in Italian the Examiners are of opinion, that she reads that language fluently, and with a good pronunciation, that she is well instructed in the grammar, translating with facility, from one language into the other. The examiners

[1] In *Pendennis* (1848–50).

think, that Miss Isabella Merritt is quite competent to teach the Italian language.

Charles Beolchi

D. Laing. M. A.
Secretary

23 Dec 1847

In the following twelve months, 118 certificates were granted altogether, more in French than in any other subject.[1] The examiners based their verdict on an assessment of performance in a viva. Some of this examining may not have been very thorough. But each candidate was given a personal report, and no two certificates bear the same wording. If the examiners had reservations, they said so. There was no fee for this examination, and the professors gave their services without payment.

The examination only served to emphasise the need for education before examination. It made more urgent the need to enlarge the horizon of these aspiring teachers.

[1] There were 36 in French, 20 in English Grammar and Literature, 12 in Scripture, 10 in Geography, 7 in Arithmetic and Euclid, 6 in Methods of teaching, 6 in Modern History, 5 in Italian, 5 in German, 4 in Drawing, 4 in Ancient History, 2 in Piano Playing, and 1 in Vocal Music.

IV

The College — Opening

1848 was a year of revolutions. Nationalism, liberalism, constitutionalism, and socialism were the words of common currency. On the continent of Europe, one revolution after another was shaking the complacency of aristocratic governments. Across the channel, Louis Philippe abdicated in February, and a republic was declared. The English Chartists were excited by these events and planned a convention for early in April; at the convention, talk of revolution was bandied about by the extremists, while the more moderate elements planned a demonstration to take place a week later. The Government recruited special constables[1] while Wellington, the commander-in-chief, moved troops into London. A feeling of alarm spread through the capital.

As it turned out, the demonstration was a fiasco. The Chartist petition, demanding the representation of the working classes in Parliament, was taken to Westminster by cab, while demonstrators calmly went home because the police barred their way northwards across the Thames from Kennington Common.

Though the Chartist movement was soon discredited, the 'condition of England' question remained. Ostensibly a movement for parliamentary reform, Chartism was prompted by frustration with the conditions of living and working in industrial England. The Chartist supporters were working-class men, many of them highly intelligent, but without political experience. Few middle- and upper-class people showed them sympathy; most were frightened of them, predicting the collapse of law and order in England if the Government yielded to their demands. Amongst the sympathisers, the most eager were Maurice and his friends.

On the day of the demonstration, April 10, Charles Kingsley[2]

[1] Maurice applied, but as a clergyman, was not accepted.

[2] Kingsley was appointed to the Committee of Education at Queen's on April 6.

was staying with Maurice, on a visit from his parish at Eversley. Maurice was ill with a bad cold, and so Kingsley went down to Waterloo Bridge to watch the events with another friend of Maurice's, John Malcolm Ludlow.[1] Discovering that there was nothing to see, they hurried home to Queen Square and sat up half the night, discussing together what they could do to help the Chartists.

They prepared a poster to put up in the streets the following day, declaring their sympathy with the demonstrators. They planned a newspaper for the working classes, designed to give 'short, pithy weekly comments on the great questions of the day in a religious spirit'. The first issue of *Politics for the People* came out on May 6 at one penny; Kingsley began his writings as 'Parson Lot'. The importance of the newspaper, as Torben Christensen has pointed out, was that for the first time the workers themselves were addressed directly by members of the middle and upper class. That the approach was not altogether appreciated is shown by the fact that only one Chartist paper made any reference to the tracts, and that the one which did put its remarks under the heading *Mock Friends of the People – Well-fed democracy in broadcloth.*[2] The newspaper did not last very long, but Maurice, always involved in practice as well as precept, took his friends into Little Ormond Yard to take night classes for working men. This in turn led to discussion groups and co-operatives and the movement known as Christian Socialism.

There are two points to be noted here. The first is that when Queen's opened, Maurice and Kingsley were largely preoccupied with the Chartist problem and Queen's did not engage their chief attention. The second is that they brought to Queen's a taint of suspicion. The more orthodox among the Established Church developed a profound suspicion of both Maurice and Kingsley. In the end Maurice was the one to suffer most, but Kingsley was the first to fall under a cloud. In this same month of April, Maurice

[1] Ludlow had been in Paris in the aftermath of the February revolution.

[2] *Commonwealth Journal*, April 27 1848. Quoted in Torben Christensen, *The Origin and History of Christian Socialism* (1962).

had approached the Council of King's to ask permission to use Kingsley as his assistant for the English Literature and History lectures. They had refused, after a special committee had met three times; Kingsley's crime was to sign articles as 'Parson Lot' and a poster addressed to 'The Workmen of England' as 'A working parson'.

Queen's first opened its doors to pupils on May 1. Almost five weeks before, on March 29, Maurice gave the Inaugural Lecture in Hanover Square Rooms—*Queen's College: its objects and method.* It is an essay on education still worth reading. Three points we will mention here. First, he defended the use of the word 'college' rather than 'school', for an establishment which was prepared to admit girls of twelve.

> The teachers of a school may aim merely to impart information; the teachers of a college must lead their pupils to the apprehension of principles . . . When I speak of leading our pupils to the study of principles, I think I mean something as nearly as possible the opposite of introducing them to an encyclopaedia of knowledge.
> . . . study is not worth much if it is not busy about the roots of things.

The idea of a college for girls was familiar; Tennyson had just published *The Princess.* Maurice referred to 'the deep wisdom which the author of *The Princess* has concealed under a veil of exquisite grace and lightness'. Tennyson was a friend of Maurice's, and it is quite possible that they had discussed such a college together. But society at large read the poem differently, and its only defence against such a revolutionary idea in practice was ridicule.

Maurice then defended the choice of subjects, of Arithmetic, Mathematics, Natural Philosophy, Languages, English Literature, Pedagogy, Mechanics, Geography, History, and Theology—and Drawing and Music, usually considered the accomplishments upon which he and others had poured scorn. The study of Drawing, he claimed, cultivates 'a power of looking below the surface of things for the meaning which they express', and Music has power to awaken 'the sense of an order and harmony in the heart of things'.

As it turned out, the Drawing classes caused perpetual trouble, and provided nothing very profound. The Music classes, on the other hand, were amongst the most successful, and had two outstanding teachers. John Hullah[1] had already started singing classes for actual or potential governesses in Highgate, and for younger girls at his home in St James' Place. He was an energetic man, 'whose existence was as nearly as possible perpetual movement', according to his wife. He was a musician and composer, and had already collaborated with Dickens in an opera called *The Village*. But his life's work was to practise and demonstrate a method of singing (Wilhem's) in which all could participate and which all could enjoy. He was encouraged by James Kay-Shuttleworth to take classes at the new Battersea Training College. Before long he was teaching at King's, Queen's, Whitelands, St Mark's and Bedford as well. He was an enthusiastic supporter of Queen's, taught there for many years, and brought his two daughter there as pupils.

The other musician, William Sterndale Bennett, was also a composer as well as a teacher. His best compositions were written when he was a very young man, and as he grew older, he gave more and more time to teaching (he finished his career as Principal of the Royal Academy of Music) and to reviving the music of Bach in England. His reputation at Queen's was not only for musicianship, but for patience. One of his pupils who later became a teacher wrote that 'in hours of irritation I used to think of Bennett, and so possessed my soul in patience'. He wrote sixty preludes and lessons 'in all the keys' especially for his Queen's pupils. His compositions are almost entirely neglected today, but his name is honoured as one who stood for the highest artistic standards, and is always associated with the revival of musical life in this country.

A third point made by Maurice in the Inaugural Lecture was that competition and the following of fashion would be avoided—a tradition which Queen's has tried to maintain to the present day:

[1] See Frances Hullah, *Life of John Hullah* (1886).

> The teacher in every department, if he does his duty, will admonish his pupils, that they are not to make fashion, or public opinion, their rule; that they are not to draw or play, or to study arithmetic, or language, or literature, or history, in order to shine or be admired; that if these are their ends, they will not be sincere in their work or do it well.

On Monday May 1, the first pupil arrived on the steps of 67 Harley Street, and was shown into the Waiting Room. She sat there debating whether or not to take off her bonnet; when the next student arrived they discussed it together, until Mrs Mattam, the Lady Resident, appeared to put them at their ease. Their bonnets came off. A little nervously, yet excited by their new adventure, they soon walked up the elegant staircase to the lecture room on the first floor.

That very first pupil, Sarah Deacon Woodman, survived to write a short article in the Jubilee History of the College in 1898. She also contributed some of her reminiscences to the College Magazine. In particular she remembered how Mrs Mattam had been able to counteract the formidable atmosphere surrounding the professors:

> How useful in her generation was that esteemed first Lady Resident, Mrs Mattam; possessed of no intellectual power nor of much organising capability, yet she proved herself the right person in the right place, for she seemed, by her almost maternal line of action, at least to understand the necessity of the moment, namely, to become the connecting link between the professors and the girls, for, though I say it with bated breath, I humbly believe that the professors were *quite* as much afraid of their girl-pupils as the girl-pupils were of them.

The first week was taken up with introductory lectures[1] by the

[1] Published as *Introductory Lectures delivered at Queen's College, London* (1849).

professors, outlining the kind of courses they were going to give. Charles Kingsley told his audience that he would hold no brief for 'extracts' or 'select beauties', but would talk about and encourage his pupils to read all kinds of English literature including modern works; he hoped that this would help them to understand 'the English spirit' and that it would help to counteract the idea that 'the minds of young women are becoming un-English'. His was a fresh and lively influence, and his lectures were very popular; one Lady Visitor complained of gate-crashers. One of the earliest pupils at Queen's remembered him electrifying the class with his retort to thoughtless opinions; 'From all hearsay and second-hand information, Good Lord deliver us.' Unfortunately he only stayed at Queen's for a short time; sometime during the following autumn he was taken ill, and was never able to resume his lectures.

We have a hint of his liberal enthusiastic approach from the letter he wrote to the Rev Alfred Strettel, who was to take his place as Professor of English Literature. The letter was written from Lynmouth and dated April 17 1849:

> Go your own way; what do girls want with a 'course of literature'? Your business and that of all teachers is, not to cram them with things but to teach them how to read for themselves. A single half century known thoroughly will give them canons and inductive habits of thought whereby to judge all future centuries. We want to train—not cupboards full of 'information' (vile misnomer), but real informed women.
>
> I quite agree with you about Chaucer's Norman and Saxon elements. I said something about it in my Introduction. Don't be afraid of talking about marriage. We must be real and daring at Queen's College, or nowhere. The 'clear stage and no favour' which we have got there is so blessed and wonderful an opening, that we must make the most of it to utter things there which prudery and fanaticism have banished from pulpits and colleges.[1]

[1] Quoted in *Charles Kingsley. His letters and memories of his life*. Ed. by his wife (1877), vol. I, p. 201.

There was another introductory lecture on Natural Philosophy given by Professor O'Brien. He accepted that he could expect no mathematical knowledge of his hearers, and therefore would have to adopt a rather general approach. He proposed to deal with Astronomy, Optics, Acoustics, Heat, Electricity, Magnetism and Mechanical Sciences. The French Professor was Isidore Brasseur, tutor to the Prince of Wales. His introductory lecture was dull and unpromising; 'the immoral tendency of most works of fiction published in our day—(a tendency which no one deplores more than myself)—makes the reading of them forbidden'. Foreign languages were taught by natives, mostly political refugees from the continent. One of the most popular and revered was Signor Fusco, who taught Italian until he was called away to help in the fight for Italian independence. Camilla Croudace later wrote that 'great was the consternation when his departure was announced'.

There was a full timetable and lectures took place from 10.0 a.m. until 3.0 p.m. (including Saturdays) without a break for lunch. The first timetable includes most of the names on the original list, together with Kingsley, O'Brien, Samuel Clark, John Hullah and Sterndale Bennett, all of whom were on the Committee of Education.

The two hundred entries in the first term showed that, despite the critics, there was a demand for the kind of education Queen's was offering. Amongst these early pupils were Dorothea Beale and her sisters, fresh from their finishing school in Paris; their brother fetched them home when the mob surrounded the school and demanded the garden tools as weapons. Dorothea had already shown a voracious appetite for education. Now she could undertake it in a systematic way. Not only did she attend many of the lectures, but she took private lessons from Professor Cock in Trigonometry, Conics and Differential Calculus. Already that independence and strength of character which was to take her to Cheltenham as Principal of the Ladies' College was demonstrated. A contemporary wrote her recollection of Dr Bernays' German class:

Dorothea and Anna Beale were once absent from the

3a The Rev R. C. Trench
Chairman of the Committee of Education 1853–63

3b The Rev E. H. Plumptre
Principal 1875–9

4a Miss Camilla
Mary Croudace
Lady Resident 1881–1906

4b The Library 1903

> German class on its first meeting for a new term. Dr Bernays said they should read Faust, and accordingly all the pupils brought copies of Faust to the next class. When all were seated, Dorothea stood up and said quietly and respectfully that she thought Faust objectionable reading for young girls, and suggested some other book. Dr Bernays looked just a little annoyed, but listened quite kindly. He said it was pity the books had been bought, but put it to the class what should be done. Such was Miss Beale's influence that all decided to submit to her judgment.[1]

Altogether Dorothea Beale took nine certificates. One was in the principles and method of teaching, and the examiners expressed their opinion that she 'promises to become an accomplished teacher'. By 1849 she had been appointed Mathematical tutor.

Teaching was soon added to the timetable, though not for very long. There was already the perennial controversy on the value of giving instruction in how to teach. In general, the Committee was anxious to concentrate on learning a subject. The general standard was so low that there was more point in improving the understanding of a subject than in discussing how to inculcate into others some barely-digested information. During the first term, the Committee of Education decided that in granting certificates they would look 'rather to the expression of the knowledge of the subject evinced, than the capability of teaching it'. From the beginning, the Committee of Education had rejected any idea of limiting the College to actual or potential governesses.

One scheme, however, was initiated especially for existing governesses; a series of evening lectures to be given free. At least six of the professors offered to give their services in this way. One of the first attenders at these classes was Frances Mary Buss, later the famous headmistress of the North London Collegiate School. She took three certificates and was given good reports. Later she wrote:

[1] Quoted in Elizabeth Raikes, *Dorothea Beale of Cheltenham* (1908), p. 420.

> Queen's College opened a new life to me, I mean intellectually. To come in contact with the minds of such men was indeed delightful, and it was a new experience to me and to most of the women who were fortunate enough to become students.

This was what Queen's meant to its first students.

V

Early Progress

THE timetable of the first term at Queen's was formidable. Altogether there were twenty-six hours of instruction on the timetable published in May 1848. Most of this was in the form of lectures, though the Modern languages classes included conversation, and the Drawing and Music classes were practical. But here it has to be remembered that for the first ten years or so the majority of pupils were non-compounders and chose their subjects and paid for them separately. In 1849, for example, there were 276 students in the College, but only 31 of these were compounders, taking the full course.

All the early pupils spoke of Maurice as the most inspiring teacher. It is extraordinary that he was able to give something to the College that it has never lost. His portraits which preside over the Library and the main corridor are symbols; they represent that integrity and breadth of outlook towards which everyone is drawn. Not only these qualities, but a respect for and enjoyment of scholarship without pedantry; and of scholarship without competition. As Camilla Croudace wrote in her *Reminiscences* in the Magazine:[1] 'He took care to let us know he did not like *cleverness*, so we did not try to be clever.' This is how she described his lectures:

> When he came into no II for literature, the room was filled to overflowing, and in the days of crinoline it was a difficult business to get into one's seat. He sat at the table where it is now placed, and began by reading the names in order, and now and then beamed a delightful smile on the front row. The roll being read, he leaned his head on his hand, and gave his lectures without notes, gently rubbing his forehead all the while as though to press out the ideas that came to

[1] Queen's College Magazine, March 1891.

> him . . . all—the serious and frivolous alike—were impressed by his strong personal influence and his intense *humility*; and his humility I think conveyed itself to his listeners; it seemed impossible to listen to Mr Maurice and to think anything of your own attainments and opinions.

As with his lectures at King's, he made no concessions to laziness and few to ignorance. Another pupil wrote: 'Pupils who came to his History lectures not familiar with the facts that were to be dealt with might feel in a mist.' Maurice did not teach History until 1856; during the first five years of the College's existence, he lectured regularly in Theology and in Mental and Moral Philosophy. There is still preserved at Queen's a half leather bound notebook kept by Louisa Twining[1] during 1849 and 1850 of Maurice's lectures on philosophy. They did not presume a previous study of the subject but they did take certain basic questions and treat them seriously and in some depth. There was, I think, little difference between them and the philosophy lectures a young student at Oxford or Cambridge might have heard during his first year. This, after all, was Maurice's life study. He spent most of his life writing two large volumes on *Moral and Metaphysical Philosophy*[2] and the last six years of his life were spent as Professor of Casuistry, Moral Theology and Moral Philosophy at Cambridge.

Caroline Fox was another adult listener to Maurice's lectures in 1849, this time on Theology. She wrote in her *Journal*[3] on one occasion: 'He was much exhausted by it, for he was thoroughly in earnest.' On another: 'Went to Harley Street to hear Maurice's lecture. It was so full and solemn that it left us all trembling with emotion.'

One thing that seems missing from Maurice's lectures is a sense of humour. They were intensely serious; also profound.

[1] Louisa Twining was then (1849) twenty-nine, and according to her own account attended lectures at Queen's for some years. Later she became a pioneer social worker. See her *Recollections of Life and Work* (1893).

[2] Published in 1861.

[3] Caroline Fox, *Memories of old friends from 1835 to 1871* (1882).

This lack of humour partly explains why he was not such a success with his students at King's. And yet in his earlier writings and in his letters to his friends it cannot be suppressed. There is a certain ironic humour, for instance, in the reply he made to Hort in a letter in that same year 1849:

> You think you do not find a distinct recognition of the devil's personality in my books. I am sorry if it is so. I am afraid I have been corrupted by speaking to a polite congregation. I do agree with my dear friend Charles Kingsley, and admire him for the boldness with which he has said that the devil is shamming dead, but that he never was busier than now.[1]

One more recollection, this time from Dorothea Beale. Maurice examined her in History and English during the first term and wrote on her certificate that she had shown 'much intelligence'. She remembered the examination with pleasure:

> The viva voce was a delightful conversation: he led us on by his sympathetic manner and kindly appreciation, so that we hardly remembered he was an examiner . . . I remember to this day what a pleasant hour we had of viva voce: his wonderful power of intellectual sympathy came out, and made us forget that we were being examined; he seemed to take pleasure in following up our thoughts on the bearings of the history we had read, so that it appeared we were holding a delightful conversation on the subject. Again, in speaking of language, he wanted not merely formal and conventional grammar, and showed such pleasure when a grammatical definition was enlarged beyond the scope of ordinary school-books.[2]

Maurice was by this time living an exceedingly busy life. He spent one whole day a week at Queen's, and one evening

[1] Quoted in J. F. Maurice, *Life of F. D. Maurice* (1884), vol. II, p. 21.
[2] Quoted in Elizabeth Raikes, *Dorothea Beale of Cheltenham* (1908) p. 27.

(Saturday) lecturing to governesses. He gave another eight lectures at King's. Added to this, he took prayers at Lincoln's Inn every day and preached there on Sundays. To his great joy he became engaged to Georgiana Hare, sister of his former teacher at Cambridge, early in 1849, and married her early in the summer. It was another very happy marriage.[1]

Another teacher who introduced a scholarly, and very serious, approach to his lectures was Richard Chenevix Trench. Trench is now probably best known as the Archbishop of Dublin who opposed the disestablishment of the Irish Church, and as the philologist who first suggested the compilation of the Oxford English Dictionary. He was a life-long scholar with wide interests. As a young man at Cambridge he had been drawn into the circle of the 'Apostles'. He was made a Professor at King's in 1846 and maintained his friendship with Maurice, so it was not surprising that he should be drawn into the circle who were to help with the Queen's project. Perhaps the fact that his own mother was a writer and poet made him especially sympathetic to the cause. He was one of the first members of the Committee of Education and began lecturing in the second term.

Every description of him notes his solemn appearance. Caroline Fox met him in 1846:

> Went to South Place to luncheon and met Dean Trench there—a large melancholy face, full of earnestness and capacity for woe. Under a portrait of himself he once found the name 'Ugolino' written, he looked so starved.

Camilla Croudace, giving her memories of these early days in the Jubilee history, gives a similar description:

> He was a most imposing personage, with a very heavy, pale face and dark eyes, and a most solemn voice, which I can still hear in imagination; and he read his lectures from a MS in a slow and impressive way. We only saw his most severe side, but I have heard that in his own

[1] His first wife had died in 1845.

home he was most amusing and delightful with young children.

One of the subjects Trench taught at Queen's was Church History. Several years later, he published his lectures on Mediaeval Church History, revised but not substantially altered. The book has twenty-nine chapters on the history of the English Church from the conversion of England to the eve of the Reformation. It was strong meat; undiluted serious history, clear but heavy. His comment on lecturing to young female students is as follows:

> I cannot think the antithesis of 'bonnets' and 'brains' to be a just one. How far the wearers of bonnets would bear the strain of competition with those thus taken to be in exclusive possession of brains, supposing the matter in hand to be one demanding originative power, on this I give no opinion; but, having regard to receptive capacity, to the power of taking in, assimilating, and intelligently reproducing, what is set before them, my conviction after some experience in lecturing to the young of both sexes is, that there is no need to break the bread of knowledge smaller for young women than for young men.[1]

Another industrious professor was Nicolay, described as 'a more facty teacher'; and not popular with everyone. He lectured on History and Geography, and his favourite expression was 'Don't you see the connection?'.

Was this institution a school or a college? In 1868, the Schools' Inquiry Commissioners listed Queen's and Bedford Colleges as the highest institutions for female education in England, comparing them with public schools for boys. In many ways this was a fair comparison. The youngest pupils at Queen's were only twelve. Those who were compounders and studied full-time followed a wide curriculum and had little opportunity for specialisation; while the majority, who were non-compounders, tended to

[1] R. C. Trench, *Lectures on mediaeval church history* (1877), Preface.

study languages, Music and Drawing and treated the College more as a finishing school. There was, of course, no established standard of entry and some students floundered during the more advanced lectures.

And yet this is not the whole story. When one looks through the list of lecturers in the first years, there are several of high academic attainment. Such a group of men would hardly have been found together in one public school. Trench and Maurice gave lectures which could equally well have been given to young men undergraduates. These lectures had a mixed audience which included several educated and discerning adults.

It seems impossible to classify Queen's accurately as either school or college. It was something unique and has remained so. For reasons which belong to its later history, its application to become a constituent member of the University of London was turned down (Bedford, on the other hand, became a part of that university) and it became the equivalent of a school, though not quite like any other school.

Until 1853 the College was still officially a branch of the Governesses' Benevolent Institution, with relations becoming a little strained as time went on. David Laing was not always the easiest person to work with. Understandably he felt touchy about the credit for Queen's going to Maurice and his friends rather than to himself. This matter came up at the August meeting of the G.B.I. Committee in 1849:

> The Hon. Sec. stated that articles had appeared in periodicals assuming for the Professors of Queen's College the credit of having established the College, and giving erroneous impressions of its cause and objects; and that he would, with the Board's permission, have an article inserted or appended to vindicate the views and claims of this society.

The other bone of contention was finance, but this was eventually amicably settled; the G.B.I. was to retain 20% of the fees for the maintenance of the building, and the rest was to go to paying the professors.

On the question of payments, it is worth noting two things.

The first is that the professors were paid well: £1 a lecture plus 6d for every pupil over the number of twenty. Considering the change in the value of money since 1848, this must be regarded as generous pay. But the second thing is that the professors, in return, were equally generous in giving their services to the College when it was necessary; they received no pay in the first five years for granting certificates, and none for the evening lectures delivered to already practising governesses. Later on they sacrificed some of their regular fees to help to establish the College on its feet.

By 1850, the G.B.I. and the Committee of Education were already discussing a legal separation of the two institutions. It took three years to complete the negotiations and it was not until November 1853 that the new charter took effect. According to this charter, the responsibility for the College was transferred to a Council, under whom the Committee of Education was to serve. The Bishop of London was appointed ex-officio Visitor of the College, a happy arrangement which still holds. The G.B.I. retained the right to nominate governesses to attend lectures at half fees, and was granted the privilege of nominating students for four free places. The two institutions now formally severed their connection, but not their interest in each other's welfare. For the next 70 years, the G.B.I. retained 66 (now 47) Harley Street as its headquarters.[1]

Another step forward was the opening of the preparatory class. The first suggestion for this came at the end of 1848, and the class was opened after Easter 1849, under the superintendence of Miss Parry. It was open to girls of nine and over, and designed to prepare them for admission to the College, some of whose students had shown themselves quite unable to benefit from the more advanced course of study there.

This class was established as a permanent feature of the College. After eighteen months Miss Parry was given an assistant, and the numbers rose the following year to forty-two. By 1852, a

[1] The G.B.I. then moved to Westminster. In 1967 it changed its name to the Schoolmistresses and Governesses' Benevolent Institution, and its present premises are in Buckingham Gate.

three-year course had been introduced. In 1860, it became known as Queen's College School, and such it has remained. Until 1898, it was housed in partitioned rooms in a converted stables in the mews at the back of the house. The present unusual division of Queen's College and School into three school classes, two junior years and two senior years goes back almost to the beginning of its history.

The difficulty with the school was in finding suitable lady staff, though the professors did help a little with the teaching. It proved a modified success. In 1865, D. R. Fearon visited the School as Assistant Commissioner of the Schools' Inquiry Commission. His report, which was published in 1868, gave a very fair and balanced assessment of Queen's. Of the School he said:

> My general impression of the school is that the pupils are backward, though not very much so, in spelling and arithmetic, and that the instruction wants more method and vigour. Some of the mistresses show very evident signs of want of training. On the whole, however, there is some good work accomplished. The school is better than the majority of private schools for girls of this social grade, though not equal to some. If more vigorously conducted it might be of very great use to the college.[1]

It is now worth asking who came to Queen's in search of education. First we might consider those for whom it was intended. The G.B.I. Committee held a discussion early in 1849 on the kind of candidates whom they would consider for free presentations. They were to be 'the daughters of professional men, that term including clergymen, barristers, solicitors, physicians, surgeons and apothecaries, of officers in the army or navy, or of such other persons in the same rank of society as the Board may deem eligible'. Frequently, Queen's was referred to as a college 'for the middle classes'. An examination of the register of pupils for the earliest years of the College shows that the students were largely confined to this section of society.

[1] *Schools' Inquiry Commission. Report 1868*, p. 581.

None were more vigilant in upholding the select nature of the clientele than the Lady Visitors. A few months after the College opened, they asked the Committee of Education to appoint a lady superintendent in the Waiting Room so that 'parents may feel secure against an indiscriminate association of different dispositions and ranks of society'. The Committee replied that 'it is a principle of the institution not to recognise any distinction of rank among the pupils'. Later on the Lady Visitors effectively crushed Nicolay's plan for an evening conversazione of students and friends of the College by objecting that 'whilst casual association in a class by no means implied association elsewhere, the meeting together in an Evening party might lead to more familiar acquaintance than parents could approve'. And in 1864 they spent the greater part of one of their meetings discussing whether the College should exclude 'the children of retail tradesmen'. They agreed that the occupation of the father should appear on all admission forms, and that 'in the case of publicans and others engaged in unsuitable callings, applicants should have a special recommendation from a member of the Council, Committee of Education or Lady Visitors.' The Committee of Education agreed to this—at the discretion of the Dean. The Schools' Inquiry Commission reported that most of the pupils at Queen's were 'upper middle class', though a certain number were 'upper class'. 'The fact, however, that the colleges[1] are only used for instruction, and not for boarding, renders a greater mixture of classes possible than would otherwise be advisable'.

The other obvious factor which would limit applications was the scale of fees. The *Quarterly Review*, in an article in March 1850, referred to 'the low rate at which every kind of instruction may here be obtained'. The Schools' Inquiry Commission, on the other hand (in 1868) made a point of commenting on the very high fees. A comparison was made between the City of London School for Boys, where the highest fees were £9 per annum; whereas both Queen's and Bedford charged between £22 and £28, with extra subjects as an additional charge. But presumably the reason for this was that all the old-established boys' schools

[1] This refers to Queen's and Bedford Colleges.

were able to lean heavily on endowments, whereas the girls' schools had to finance themselves entirely out of the fees charged. As time went on, scholarships were established; but in the earliest years, the only free places available were those under the presentation of the G.B.I.

So the College was established and launched on its way. Though it has never become a large institution, and has had many difficult periods to work through, it has shown remarkable powers of survival. In the next chapter, we will consider some of the early criticisms and crises which it had to experience.

VI

Early Difficulties

MAURICE was a controversial figure. He was too original and too outspoken to avoid criticism, and seemed almost to attract controversy. He had already clashed with his college authorities at King's on several occasions; one of these, we have already noted, was over the appointment of Kingsley as his assistant lecturer. He also found himself in trouble with the Press.

Maurice had always deplored the custom of the unsigned article, which became the vehicle of scurrilous and bitter vendettas. He once wrote to Kingsley:

> You know that the *we* covers the most insolent pretension, the most offhand dogmatism, the most haughty scorn of individuals and of mankind.

In the 1840s and 1850s he became the victim of such attacks, and they landed him in serious trouble.

The *Quarterly Review* was an important literary journal of Tory leanings. One of its more notorious contributors was J. Wilson Croker, whom Macaulay 'detested more than cold boiled veal'. From 1848, Queen's College and its founder drew venom from its pages. It started quite mildly in December 1848, with a review of the 1847 Report of the G.B.I.:

> . . . as the zeal and highest responsibility and recommendation of an *English* governess must even rest more upon her moral than her literary qualifications, the plan of subjecting her to an examination on the latter appears to us neither wise nor fair. This plan, it is true, has been pursued with tolerable success abroad, but it must be kept in mind that the foreign governess is a mere teacher, whose duties cease with the school-room hours, who has her three months' holiday in the year, and who has, in short, little or nothing

to do with the moral guidance of her pupils. What we, on the contrary, require and seek for our children is not a learned machine stamped and ticketed with credentials like a piece of patent goods, but rather a woman endowed with that sound principle, refinement and sense, which no committee of education in the world could ascertain or certify.

There followed much more serious criticism in March 1850,[1] in another review of a G.B.I. Report and of the *Introductory Lectures*. The main criticism was against the religious teaching:

> . . . we think no critic can fail to detect in this volume traces of a school of so-called theology which seems to be gaining ground among us—a sort of modified pantheism and latitudinarianism—a system not of bringing religion into everything, but of considering everything as more or less inherently religious.

Quotations were given from Maurice's lecture to illustrate the point. The other lecturer who was singled out was Kingsley:

> . . . this Lecturer on English Composition, we may observe in passing, distinguishes himself even above the rest of this company by the Germanisms embroidered on his prose—another indication of leanings that require to be watched.

They deplored Kingsley's emphasis on developing the imagination:

> If ever poor mortal needed to have imagination kept under control, and plain practical common sense largely developed, as a safeguard alike for her feelings and her conduct, it is the governess.

Maurice immediately replied to this article in a *Letter to the*

[1] *Quarterly Review*, vol. 86, March 1850, pp. 364–82.

Bishop of London.[1] He accepted the criticism of the organisation of the College (this was before the charter) but fiercely rejected the rest. He pointed out that if heresy was being taught at Queen's, then it was also being taught at King's. This, unfortunately, was the conclusion arrived at three years later by the majority of the Council of King's College.

In the following September, Kingsley published *Alton Locke*, a novel exposing some of the evils of contemporary society; it brought him further notoriety. This time it was the *Record* which launched an attack, in a letter signed 'Presbyter E', warning those who might consider sending their daughters to Queen's that they ought to know 'the nature of the influences under which young and susceptible minds are likely to be brought in that institution'.[2] The *Record* was one of the two journals of the Evangelical party in the Church of England. Owen Chadwick has distinguished between the two in this way: 'Of their two journals, the *Christian Observer* practised charity and had few subscribers, the *Record* acted vituperative partisan and had many subscribers.'[3] On this occasion the *Record* did not confine itself to an attack on Kingsley but brought in Maurice as well. Meanwhile Nicolay, enthusiastic for the cause of Queen's but tactless in his methods, wrote an article in the *Record* explaining that Kingsley no longer belonged to the College. Maurice read it, and was soon at his desk; he could not bear compromise or dissimulation, and thought that Nicolay's article hinted at both. He wrote as follows:

21, Queen Square.
Nov. 11 1850.

My dear Nicolay,

I read on Saturday in the Record a letter signed Presbyter N. I cannot doubt that it is yours. You say in it that you have given your name to the Editor. Of course therefore he

[1] *Letter to the Lord Bishop of London, in reply to the article in no 172 of the Quarterly Review* (1850).
[2] October 1850.
[3] In *The Victorian Church*, vol. I (1966), p. 448.

is aware that you are the Deputy Chairman of the Committee of Education. In this letter you state the fact that Kingsley has not done any work in Queen's College for two years. You clearly leave the impression on the mind of a reader that the tendency of his late book is such as to make us glad that he is not connected with us. I am sure that inference will be drawn from what you have said by the Editor of the Paper and by all who take any interest in the subject.

Now I have little doubt that a majority of the Committee of Education would agree with you in the opinion which you have thus expressed or indicated. If any should differ with you they are fairly entitled to look upon it merely as a question of taste or feeling which does not affect their position in the College at all. My case is entirely different. I am pledged to a cause which makes it very important that I should not even appear to think a book evil which I believe to be working heart and soul for a great, unpopular, necessary object. I shall of course be asked privately and perhaps publicly Do you as Chairman of the Committee subscribe to the opinion of that letter. If I answer, No, as I must do, it will be felt that we have been cheating the public. The person whose name stands most prominently in your paper does not abide by the sentiment which you have put forward and which was intended to give confidence—and will give confidence—to the minds of your supporters.

A disclaimer of your opinion—even a modification of it or an explanation of any kind would be most unpleasant to me and might be ruinous to the College. On any ground I should avoid that course especially because I believe your letter was well intended and well timed and because I know it will have quieted the minds of some who were asked to be members of the future Council.

There is therefore but one course open to me. I must request you to inform the committee that I resign my place in it and that I shall only continue my lectures in the College till the end of the present term.

Your letter has only made it clear to me *when* I ought to

take this step. I have felt for a long time on quite different grounds that I must take it sooner or later. The objections which have been made to my teaching and to my opinions are far more serious than any which have been raised against Kingsley; they must affect the College more because I have had, nominally, a more conspicuous place in it and the public could not know how small the classes are over which I have had any direct influence. From the experience I have had of the great kindness of my colleagues, I know that if they were suffering ever so much from my connexion with them, they would not turn me out. It becomes therefore more especially my duty to take the matter into my own hands. I should have done so last Easter if it had not appeared right to face the storm which the Quarterly raised rather than to retire from it. Had I followed my judgment rather than my inclination or vanity I should have resigned at the beginning of this Session. Some remarks of my colleagues at King's College proved to me that I could not long delay with safety to your institution; I am thankful that this Record controversy has obliged me to come to an immediate decision.

I have made this statement first to show that I have taken my resolution deliberately and that no expression of kind regret on the part of colleagues can change it, secondly to prove that you are not in the least to blame for the letter you have written and that it is only the accidental cause of my retiring from the College, thirdly to make it evident that my case is entirely peculiar and that no other member of the Committee ought to consider himself in any sense affected by my conduct, lastly that I may leave no doubt in any of your minds how thoroughly I am interested in the great work in which you are engaged and how cordially and affectionately I take leave of them whom I have been permitted to help in it. May God prosper it to them.

Very truly yours,

F. D. MAURICE[1]

[1] MS letter in the possession of Queen's College.

Two days later, Maurice wrote to Nicolay again:

21, Queen Square
Nov. 13 1850

My dear Nicolay,

I need not reply to that part of your kind letter in which you justify your own intentions in writing to the Record. It is quite satisfactory; but on that point I was satisfied already. I still think that the Editor and readers of the paper will hold me committed to a certain disapprobation of Kingsley's book & of his opinions and I wish it clearly to be understood that I do not feel that disapprobation, but sympathise with him & desire to work with him.

I cannot agree with that part of your letter which refers to my own position in Queen's College & so much exaggerates the importance of it; though of course I am very much gratified by such expressions of kindness from any colleague, especially from one who was so instrumental in establishing our Institution, at a time when I was lukewarm or hopeless about it.

One passage in your letter has had great weight with me. It is that in which you say that the retirement of Kingsley and myself will lead working men to think that the other clergymen have endeavoured, and I can bear him witness that he has still more strenuously, to make just the opposite impression on our minds, to convince them that the clergy generally, however they may differ with us about particular plans, desire their well being and well doing heartily and must be enthusiastically the leaders in any great movement for the improvement of their condition moral or physical. If any act of mine tended in the slightest degree to alienate them from the clergy or indeed from any class of their countrymen, I should look upon that act as a sin to be repented of.

Upon considering the whole subject & giving the weight to your arguments and those of other friends which they ought to have, in spite of the partiality which dictates them, I have determined that the proper course for me to take is this. I wish you to lay my resignation before the Committee of Education & to say that I regard it as absolute; but that if they wish me to retain the office of Chairman till the new Council is appointed, it being understood that they or they & you conjointly have the power of filling it up just as they please, I am quite ready to do so. If the Council choose me for the office ultimately I will accept it; for they will take that course with their eyes open & I am not answerable for their mistakes. The question of my continuing on the Committee and continuing to lecture I look upon as quite subordinate. I doubt whether it is advisable that the class on Moral Philosophy should be kept up as it is so small & will probably become smaller. But that is a point which I do not wish to decide & I shall be always glad to give the Evening lectures to Governesses.

Believe me,
My dear Nicolay,
Yours very truly,
F. D. MAURICE[1]

For the time being, Maurice agreed to stay. Kingsley, however, resigned from the Committee of Education. He was no longer teaching at the College, and if the association of his name with that of Queen's was doing it harm, the sooner the official connection was severed, the better.

The following year there was more trouble. The *Quarterly Review*[2] included in its September issue a scathing indictment of both Maurice and Kingsley:

> Incredible as it may appear, there is, it seems, a clique of educated and clever, but wayward-minded men—the most prominent of them, two *clergymen of the Church of England*—who from, as it seems, a morbid craving for notoriety or

[1] MS letter in the possession of Queen's College.
[2] In an article on *Revolutionary Literature* by J. Wilson Croker.

> a crazy straining after paradox have taken up the unnatural and unhallowed task of preaching, in the press and from the pulpit, not indeed such open, undisguised *Jacobinism and jacquerie* as we have just been quoting, but, under the name of *Christian Socialism*, the same doctrines in a form not the less dangerous for being less honest.

The Principal and the governors of King's were alarmed enough to call a special committee. After careful discussion they declared their confidence in Maurice.

That confidence lived just two more years. It is ironic that the college that has recently established an F. D. Maurice Chair of Moral and Social Theology should have expelled him from its ranks at the height of his career. But this is what happened. In 1853 Maurice was dismissed from his Chair of Divinity at King's. The same month, he resigned from the Chairmanship of the Committee of Education at Queen's.

Maurice had given some theological lectures in Lincoln's Inn, and they were published as *Theological Essays* in the summer of 1853. He knew they would cause trouble, for he confided to Kingsley: 'I knew when I wrote the sentences about eternal death, that I was writing my own sentence at King's College.' He had attacked the current popular view of the endlessness of future punishment and maintained that 'eternal' in the New Testament had nothing to do with time.[1] When he wrote about eternal life, or eternal death, he was writing about a quality of life; eternal life was life supernatural and timeless, eternal death was its negation. He believed this passionately and fervently, and defended to the last his right to say so. The Principal of King's, Dr Jelf, was a kind man but a narrow theologian of rigid views; he believed steadfastly in rewards and punishments, and in eternal damnation. When the Council of King's noted that Maurice's views showed 'a dangerous tendency' and when the *Reasoner* and the *Inquirer* joined in the fray, Jelf, already in

[1] New Testament scholars today would agree with Maurice's interpretation.

doubt about Maurice's orthodoxy, found no way of defending him. Although both Gladstone and Bishop Wilberforce attempted to mediate in the dispute, it was of no avail. In November, Maurice was dismissed.

On November 10, Maurice wrote to Nicolay:

> My dear Nicolay,
>
> So far as I can see at present the right course respecting my relation to Queen's College is this.
>
> 1. To give up the Chairmanship of the Committee of Education formally if the deed requires it, tacitly if that is legally sufficient.
>
> 2. To accept the two lectureships in English Literature and Moral Philosophy provided the Council *unanimously* wishes me to do so after the question has been fairly and formally submitted to them and they have considered the pros and cons of it. I mean that my name should not be merely allowed to pass among the rest who will be reelected as a matter of course, but that the difficulties should be stated to the Council & that they should do what they do, with their eyes open; a single black ball to exclude. If there is not a full meeting the first time, I think the subject had better be adjourned and made special, though on that point I do not wish to insist. I should think that Trench as senior Clergyman on the Committee should be asked to be Chairman; I think he could attend often and when he did not you could always fill his place. This arrangement I think will be acceptable to the Council & will explain itself.
>
> In no case will I subject myself, as at present advised, to rejection by the Bishop or undertake to represent the Committee before the Council.
>
> Very truly yours,
>
> F. D. MAURICE[1]

[1] MS letter in the possession of Queen's College.

And on November 11:

21, Queen Square
Nov. 11 1853

My dear Nicolay,

Is the meeting on Tuesday before or after the meeting of the Council?

I believe you are mistaken about the result of the course I have taken. The sentiments of the Bishop I do not know. Browne & Hall I think would rather be rid of me. Garnier I may almost say I *know* would. If therefore my plan is faithfully pursued & I cannot admit any deviation from it, my opinion is that I shall die by the hands of the Council. But I have no wish to die by my own. It is a sadder thing to me, in some ways, to part with that which I have watched from its birth than to be cast out of such an Institution as King's College.

I will write to Trench by this post.

Very truly yours,

F. D. MAURICE[1]

On November 14, the Council of Queen's College met for the first time under its new Charter. A majority favoured Maurice's continuing to lecture at the College, but a minority did not. When Maurice heard the result, he wrote to the Committee of Education and had the letter delivered to their meeting the next day.

21, Queen Square
Nov. 15 1853

My dear Friends,

You will allow me, I am sure, to dispense with ordinary formalities in bidding farewell to the Committee of Education with which I have worked so happily for nearly six years.

When I was dismissed from King's College I felt that I might subject you to serious misrepresentations from the

[1] MS letter in the possession of Queen's College.

public & perhaps to a rebuke from the Visitor if I remained among you.

I did not however feel that I should be justified in resigning altogether & I understood it to be the wish of many, perhaps most of you, that I should not.

I took this course. I announced to the Deputy Chairman that if I was elected unanimously by the Council, I would continue to lecture in the College on Moral Philosophy & English Literature, but that if there was any dissentient voice I should act as if I were rejected. I said, at the same time, that under no circumstances could I retain the office of Chairman of your Committee. It seemed to me a very different thing to be a teacher in the College and to represent the body of its teachers before the Council & the Visitor.

It has been announced to me that a majority of the Council, at their meeting yesterday, were in favour of my continuing to hold my lectureships, but that there were dissentients who stated their reasons for thinking that I ought to be dismissed. I am therefore bound in honour to fulfil the promise I gave in my letter to Mr Nicolay, which, at my request, he communicated to the Council.

But were I free from that obligation I should still feel that I could not be the one Teacher in the College upon which this stigma has been fixed, the single person who would be presented to the Visitor under a protest from members of the Council to whose opinion he would probably attach great weight. I should be putting myself in a dishonourable position; what is of much more importance, I should be bringing you, who have kindly given my name a prominence to which it was not entitled, into unfair suspicion.

There is therefore but one course open to me. I am thankful that the sharp pain which it costs me to sever a connexion so affectionate & cordial as ours has been will not be increased by the reflection that the College will be a sufferer. Previously to the appointment of a Council even a single withdrawal might have shaken you; now I trust you will become stronger every day. My Moral Philosophy class though it has increased this term is still the smallest in the College; in Literature I was merely acting as Strettel's substitute. The Office of Chairman you will be able to supply admirably, even if the zeal and efficiency of the excellent Deputy did not make it now, as it has always been, a very easy office. What a pleasant one your confidence has made it, I do not trust myself to say even in a letter; I had not courage to tell you in person this evening.

I wish I could leave behind me some token of my affection to an institution which I have had the great honour and privilege of watching from its birth. I fear I must be content with asking you to consider my share of the fund raised for paying for the Charter and for discharging our obligations to the Governesses' Society as the property of the College.

Ever, my dear Friends,

Affectionately yours,

F. D. MAURICE[1]

Formal letters of valediction followed. His pupils presented Maurice with a silver inkstand. The Committee of Education wanted to commission a painting of Maurice to hang up in the College, a proposal which he declined; it would give the College bad publicity, for 'it would be absurd to pretend ignorance of the fact that I am regarded with suspicion—I might use a much stronger word—by a number of those who may hereafter send their children to the College, probably by a number of those whose children are there now.' Maurice's portrait was hung in the College; but not yet.

Maurice had 'set the keystone to the arch', as Trench put it, of the first college for female education. For the next three years, he did not visit the houses in Harley Street to give lectures, and his interest in education found an outlet in the establishment of the Working Men's College in Red Lion Square. Richard Trench took his place as chairman of the Committee of Education.

[1] MS letter in the possession of Queen's College, quoted in J. F. Maurice, *Life of F. D. Maurice* (1884), vol. II. pp. 215–16.

Maurice did come back in 1856 and lectured at Queen's for another ten years. But when he left in 1853, the first stage of the history of the College was over.

The difficulties at Queen's were not confined to attacks by outsiders, or to the unpopularity of Maurice with the Anglican Establishment. Nicolay and the Lady Visitors were drawn into an attitude of mutual suspicion, culminating in a series of resignations in 1856.

A distinctive feature of Queen's, for better or for worse, was that the organisation and teaching in the College were almost entirely in the hands of men for at least half a century; women were given a subsidiary role as tutors and Lady Visitors. There was a male Principal until 1931. In the 1850s the male Committee of Education, supported by the Council, took the important decisions, while the Lady Visitors were left to pass on suggestions in writing for the Committee's consideration. The trouble was that there was no proper channel of communication between the two groups, and at one stage there was practically an open declaration of war between them.

The Lady Visitors were formidable adversaries, thirty or so in number. Amongst those who left their mark were Lady Stanley of Alderley, the Lady Monteagle, Lady Caroline Stirling, Emily Taylor and Mrs Hensleigh Wedgwood. Dorothea Beale remembered two of these with pleasure: 'Lady Stanley of Alderley, stately and beautiful all her life, but especially then: Mrs Wedgwood, the daughter of Sir James Mackintosh, so clever and kind, whom everybody liked!' Lady Stanley was one of the doyens of the women's education movement; she was active in the formation of Girton, the Girls' Public Day School Company and the London School of Medicine for Women. She did not confine her interests to education, for Palmerston referred to her as the joint whip, with her husband, of the Whig party.[1]

[1] See her article, *Personal recollections of women's education*, in *The Nineteenth Century* (1879), pp. 308–21.

The arrangement was that they would attend each class or lecture according to a rota, and would meet regularly to discuss the problems which arose. The rota was drawn up, but there was no means of enforcing it. Attendance varied; on the whole it was more regular at the lectures than at classes because they were more interesting.

We have already referred to the locked book in which the Lady Visitors noted their ideas or grievances. Early in 1849, Emily Taylor wrote in it:

> It has struck me since my connection with the College as a Visitor, that there is a want of some more direct, distinct communication between the Committee of Education and the Ladies Visitors with regard to any plans determined on by the former . . . If they were made aware distinctly what is intended to be done, before it is actually put in execution, instead of leaving it to be guessed at or inferred, I believe it would be better.

Nicolay (the Dean) wrote in reply that 'the Committee are most anxious to offer the greatest facilities of co-operation to the Ladies Visitors'. The Committee was well-disposed towards the Lady Visitors, but the fact that they never met together until a sub-committee was formed in 1874 made communication difficult and open to misunderstanding.

Often the Lady Visitors made irritating and unenlightened suggestions. The wife of the Bishop of Bombay suggested that

> books of fiction, whether novels or idle tales, should be prohibited, and that elder students, who choose to bring such for their amusement *en route* to the College, should be required to leave them in charge of the porter, and not about the lecture or reception rooms, where they are calculated to prove a temptation to young and unstable students.

The Committee refrained from making any general rule along these lines. But on the whole the Lady Visitors concerned themselves with familiar essential details—proper ventilation, supplies of slates and pencils, and attention being given to the lecture taking place rather than in preparation for the next one.

In 1851, they protested vigorously that the Committee of Education and G.B.I. should carry out their promise of a reform in the government of the College:

> they . . . desire to express the strong opinion they entertain of the necessity of such improvement, and to add, that they shrink from the responsibility of continuing to give their names as visitors, unless some such change can be carried out.

The following year, they made strong objections to the discontinuance of lectures on 'method', which had been given for four years by Samuel Clark, now Principal of Battersea Training College. Yet one sensed the dilemma of the Professors, when they wrote that method lectures were in danger 'of becoming an instrument of criticism in the method of teaching adopted by the other professors of the college'.

The real crisis came in the winter of 1855–6, when the owner of the house next door to 67 Harley Street died and the lease became available. It offered just the extra accommodation the College needed, and would in addition make it possible to have resident students. The purchase of the lease was soon arranged, and plans made for the use of the new house. The Committee of Education asked the Lady Visitors whether they favoured a resident Principal, Dean or Superintendent. The Lady Visitors decided that a resident lady was necessary; some, but not all of them, agreed to the residence of a married man, an official connected with the College, provided that there was no direct communication between his quarters and the boarders' apartments.

One suspects that Nicolay seized with alacrity the chance of taking up residence at Queen's. We noted earlier that he suffered from feelings of inferiority, and here was a chance to raise his status and reach perhaps nearer to the position of Principal which he may have coveted. Had the suggested occupant of 68 been Maurice, both the Committee of Education and the Lady Visitors would have been highly satisfied. They had already said so. But Nicolay was a different matter, and his application for residence presented a problem.

The Lady Visitors did not like Nicolay. One reason they gave for opposing his tenancy of 68 was that he had eight children of both sexes, the eldest being a boy of fourteen. 'The objections which the Lady Visitors raised to the occupation of the upper floors of no 68 by any person having a family of children, some of whom might be growing into manhood, were founded upon moral considerations.' They also disliked his habit of interviewing pupils alone, and, they alleged, of exerting pressure upon them to take certain subjects and abandon others. They passed a resolution to the Committee of Education:

> They request to know whether they may depend upon *no interview* taking place in future between a *professor* and a *pupil* without the presence of the Lady Superintendent—or of a tutor, Lady Visitor or Mother of the Pupil.

In addition, they expressed a lack of confidence in his 'truthfulness and straightforwardness of dealing' and in his 'delicacy and tact as the Head of a College for Female Education'.

The Council, with whom the final decision rested, heard statements from the Committee of Education and the Lady Visitors, and could not agree with their lack of trust in Nicolay. They therefore accepted the recommendation of the Committee of Education and offered part of 68 to Nicolay at a rent of £80 per annum. That was in June. In September, twenty-one of the Lady Visitors resigned, on the grounds that 'the Council and Committee of Education . . . have wholly disregarded that control over the domestic arrangements and moral discipline of the College, with which the Lady Visitors are expressly charged.'

One of the Council members, Becket Denison (his wife was a Lady Visitor) wrote to the Principal, Trench:

> So the fatal blow is struck, and Mrs Galton and Mrs James and their long tail abandon QCL to its fate. They have sent

> to ask my wife to join and have got the answer which they might expect. But what I write for is to express the hope that no kind of argumentation or expostulatory or even regretful answer may be sent to them, but simply an acknowledgement, and a statement that their names shall henceforward be omitted from the list of Lady Visitors as they desire. Of course steps must be taken to find some new ones; it will not be easy to find more mischievous ones than the leaders of this faction.

In November Dorothea Beale resigned. She had been tutor to the I Juniors in Arithmetic and Latin for five and three years respectively, and for two years, assistant to the superintendent of the preparatory class. Her complaint against Nicolay was his private discouragement of pupils to attend many of the classes; in general, she complained of superficial teaching and the lack of female supervision. This was a great loss, though there was no suitable position for someone of her talent to look to in the future. Within two years, she was headmistress of Cheltenham Ladies' College.

In December, Nicolay himself resigned as Dean and left the premises at no 68. Just over a year later he resigned altogether, and accepted a post as chaplain in Bahia, in South America. He left under something of a cloud, though his memory obscured some of the details of his career at Queen's, and he was happy to assume, in retrospect, responsibility for the foundation of Queen's. How fair were the charges against him? The Council and Committee of Education never accepted the charges of the Lady Visitors, but they did refer more than once to 'defects of temper'. He was tactless, had an inferiority complex, and overreached himself in applying for residence at Queen's. The real tragedy was that Maurice had resigned in 1853 and was never able to take the position of Principal.

VII

The Place of Queen's in the Early Development of Women's Education

QUEEN'S was the first institution for the higher education of women to be established in the nineteenth century. It was closely followed, within eighteen months, by the opening of the Ladies' College, Bedford Square—now Bedford College in the University of London. The Ladies' College was organised along very similar lines to Queen's. It is now worth examining the connection between these two colleges.

The moving spirit behind Bedford College was Mrs Reid, a widow who was a leading figure in Abolitionist and Unitarian circles in London, and a close friend of Henry Crabb Robinson. According to her own account, she had made several attempts to establish a college for women before 1848, all of which failed 'for want of co-operation'. No details of these attempts survive. In 1847 she tried a new method. She wrote a letter to Lady Romilly:

> containing the startling announcement that half a dozen worthy gentlemen had met at breakfast at a friend's house and there had discussed the very unsatisfactory state of women's education. The letter went on to say that these worthy gentlemen, conscience-stricken at the thought of the advantages of education they had over their sisters, determined to see if something could be done to mend matters . . .
> It soon appeared that these wealthy and conscience-stricken gentlemen were myths, conjured up by the writer of the aforesaid letter, Mrs Reid, who thought by this harmless device she could best introduce a scheme she had formed.[1]

Lady Romilly (whose father was the first principal of King's)

[1] *Bedford College Magazine*, March 1887.

was impressed, and was soon a Lady Visitor at Queen's, and one of Mrs Reid's helpers in the foundation of Bedford.

Mrs Reid was a Unitarian, and moved in less orthodox circles than the founders of Queen's. She wanted her college to be different from Queen's in two ways. First, she intended to include women in the government of the college from the beginning. Secondly, she wanted the college to be undenominational rather than Anglican. But she sought help from supporters of Queen's; the first prospectus of Bedford stated that the success of Queen's showed that a demand for such education existed, and that Bedford 'has the cordial encouragement and approbation of several of the most influential members of Queen's College'.

Mrs Reid's staunchest supporter at the beginning was Francis Newman, younger brother of John Henry Newman. Francis Newman was the Professor of Latin at University College, a dissenter and later a freethinker. 'To be in direct conflict with current opinion, he himself said was to be in his element.'[1] He published a book in 1850, *Phases of Faith*, which raised a similar storm of protest to Maurice's *Theological Essays*, though for different reasons. In it, Newman rejected 'accepted religion' and virtually declared himself a freethinker. In face of the storm, he offered to resign, but was persuaded to stay. It was his association with the college which caused Maurice to refuse to be connected with it. Nicolay, however, had no such qualms, and allowed himself to be appointed Professor of Biblical Teaching; he also gave the Inaugural Lecture. But then Jelf stepped in and forbade him, as a member of the King's College staff, to teach in a college which had so many dissenters amongst the lecturers. Both John Hullah and Sterndale Bennett appear amongst the staff for the first term.

Bedford copied the Queen's tradition of Lady Visitors, and several amongst them officiated in both establishments. These included Mrs Hensleigh Wedgwood and Lady Romilly. The age of entry was fixed at twelve, as at Queen's. In 1853, a school was opened to form preparatory classes to the college, and the governess to the school was Frances Martin, a former Queen's student

[1] H. Hale Bellot, *University College, London. 1826–1926* (1929).

who later became Principal of the Working Women's College, founded by Maurice (the College was later renamed the Frances Martin College).

The syllabus was much the same as Queen's. In the first term, sixty-eight students enrolled. It did not immediately flourish and Mrs Reid was disappointed. She wrote to Henry Crabb Robinson:

> If they could but see and feel, as I do, that we shall never have better Men till men have better Mothers, they would come flocking about us.

Eventually it did flourish, and was admitted as a constituent member of the University of London at the beginning of this century.

It seems that Mrs Reid's policy of involving women much more fully in the organisation of the college paid dividends. It made for a more effective educational community, and though the Professors were not always *persona grata* with the Lady Visitors, there was not such friction as at Queen's. Mrs Reid herself was determined that control should remain in the hands of women, and before she died, she left a financial trust for the college, to be administered by three unmarried women trustees.

In 1854, Queen's invited Bedford to send delegates to a meeting to 'agree upon some united course of action concerning the Ladies' Colleges'. A few months earlier a sub-committee at Queen's had discussed the possibility of a union between Queen's, Bedford, Hyde Park College and the City College. (The City College was formed in 1849 as a branch of Queen's at 4 Artillery Place, and survived until the beginning of the present century. The organisation and timetable were modelled on those of Queen's, and David Laing, Nicolay and Miles Beale were amongst the committee.) The meeting held in 1854 was friendly, and it was agreed that a basis for union already existed in the examinations for certificates. It was suggested that the board of examiners should include representatives from each college.

There was much talk of this project of Schools in Union in the 1850s, but it had little effect, and the proposals were taken no further, although other schools applied, and elaborate terms were drawn up. It was suggested that Queen's might issue certificates to pupils from other schools, but this did not develop into any significant project. The initiative in leading the movement for women's education now came from other circles.

Miss Buss wrote in a letter to her great contemporary, Dorothea Beale: 'Queen's College began the Women's Education Movement undoubtedly, but it grew conservative . . .' This we have to admit is true. Queen's remained a relatively isolated institution, and as a college, it did not lead any movement for the extension of educational opportunities for women.

There were people who believed that Queen's could lead the way, and urged the College to do so. Miles Beale (Dorothea's father) a loyal and enthusiastic supporter of 'the women's education movement', wrote to Plumptre, regretting that the College was not doing more:

> 31, Finsbury Sq.
> June 22 1857.
>
> Rev and dear Sir,
>
> Your notion that the Universities might act in the matter of female education has surprised me—I cannot yet believe the older Universities prepared to step so far forward to meet the requirements of the time—still less can I conceive they would act with the London University.
>
> The formation of a Board of the first men in their respective departments of science, and no professor examining pupils from his own school, has seemed to me, for years, the measure most calculated to raise the status and remuneration of the Governess and secure the public from ignorance and pretension.
>
> The Queen's College: as soon as possessed of a charter, was apparently in a position to carry out these views—immediately after it was recognised to this extent, I was one, who waited upon its Com: to know upon what terms it would affiliate with kindred societies—suffice it to say its views appeared to that deputation too narrow to be beneficial to the public. Since that time, I have thought much and conversed with others upon the subject. I enclose you

two letters from Dr Carpenter—from one of the Examiners of the Ctte of education—I met with much encouragement. I joined myself to the Society of Arts, because it was the only body I found ready to act.

I am very desirous to see some body recognised by the Governm. granting certificates equivalent to degrees. I cannot but believe that Q. Coll. has sufficient influence, if conducted upon more liberal views, to secure this standing to the Governess, with every advantage to the Institution itself, whilst delay would seem to threaten the establishment of some less effective board.

Rev and dear Sir,
Your very obt servant,
MILES BEALE[1]

Another person who wanted Queen's to lead the way in securing university admission for women was Emily Davies,[2] the founder of Girton College. She and her favourite brother, Llewelyn, had fallen under the influence of Maurice and wanted to help with his educational projects. She was involved in the movement for women's suffrage in the 1860s, had already petitioned London University to admit women to degrees, and formed a committee to press for the admission of girls to Oxford and Cambridge Local Examinations.

A Miss Drewry had written to Queen's in 1861 urging the Committee of Education to press for the opening of the examinations to girls, but 'the committee decided that it was not at present desirable for them to take any steps in the matter'.

Emily Davies began her campaign for the admission of women to local examinations in 1862. She wrote to both Oxford and Cambridge Boards; each refused, but Cambridge was the more encouraging. She formed a committee, and wrote for help to influential friends. One of them, Dyke Acland, sent a reply typical of many men who were anxious to be helpful but fearful of the results of such dangerous requests:

[1] MS letter in the possession of Queen's College.
[2] See Barbara Stephen, *Emily Davies and Girton College* (1927).

> If publicity and freedom be by the general consent of educated men necessary to the full development of boys' nature, a certain degree of privacy and clinging for protection is equally indispensable for the full ripening of the precious qualities of womanhood. I confess therefore that I feel a shrinking indisposition to throw the girls of England into public competition with the boys.[1]

In 1863, when Cambridge organised an experimental examination for girls, several students from Queen's were entered, though the attitude of the Committee of Education was cautious. At their meeting on November 17 1863:

> The Dean reported that 18 or 20 pupils of the College had intimated their intention to offer themselves for the examination held in connexion with the syndicate of the University of Cambridge for local Examinations, and was requested to inform Miss Davies, the Lady acting as Honorary Secretary of the London Committee for organising such Examination, that while the Committee had not thought it right to interpose any obstacle to the carrying into execution of the pupils' intentions in this matter they had left them to do so, at the discretion of their parents, without selecting any picked candidates or giving them any special training.

The following year, a petition, or memorial, was prepared on the subject to be sent to the university authorities. Again the Committee of Education was cautious:

> The Dean having submitted a memorial proposed to be sent to the Vice Chancellor and Senate of the University of Cambridge, requesting the extension to girls of the system of local examinations, it was resolved, that the Committee are not prepared to take any corporate action on the matter

[1] Quoted in Barbara Stephen, *Emily Davies and Girton College* (1927), p. 85.

> but leave it to the professors to sign or not at their discretion.

In fact, seventeen of the staff signed the memorial.

Miss Davies, like Miss Beale, was very anxious that Queen's should lead the way in providing a properly recognised university education for women. Plumptre was her friend at Queen's, and she wrote to him in September 1866:

> I find among the higher class of schoolmistresses in all parts of the country a strong disposition to put themselves into friendly relations with the London Colleges. They would like their schools to be to the Colleges what the Public Schools are to the Universities, but with that view they want the Colleges to be *really* places of higher education than schools can be. Hitherto they have been more like rival schools. In fact I have heard of a case in which a girl was sent first to College, and then to school to finish. I do not see how this can be got over excepting by raising the age of the College students and giving them some higher kind of examination than any that is open to schools. I believe there would be no difficulty in getting these from Cambridge, if the Colleges are willing to accept what the University has to give, that is, the examinations for Ordinary Degrees . . . It seems to me that this kind of affiliation to Cambridge would in the case of Queen's College be much more satisfactory than anything we are likely to get from the London University, and I am sure it would make the College much more popular with the schools and more looked up to in the country generally than it now is. I am afraid Bedford College will be shut out by its constitution, as the Cambridge Little-Go examination includes some little Theology and at Bedford College they get over the religious difficulty by excluding it. I suppose Greek is more likely to be the stumbling-block at Queen's.[1]

[1] Quoted in Barbara Stephen, *Emily Davies and Girton College* (1927), p. 146.

Again, Emily Davies' efforts to stir up Queen's met with no success. Plumptre replied:

> I doubt whether it would be wise to raise the age limit of admission until public opinion has ripened on the matter of employment for women.

This was a reference to the suspicion and prejudice which surrounded the Society for Promoting the Employment of Women.

In 1866, the post of Assistant Secretary at Queen's fell vacant. Plumptre had told Emily Davies of the vacancy, and she interpreted his letter as an invitation to apply. She wrote in her diary:

> My idea was that if I were inside the place, I might be able to help forward some plan for the affiliation of the College to the University of Cambridge, which at that time was our modest aspiration.

There was an odd result of her application. She and the other seven applicants were interviewed by a sub-committee; four votes were given to Emily Davies, and three to Mary Jane Milward. Yet when the Council met to interview these two candidates, the vote was given unanimously to Miss Milward. One suspects of the Council a conservative prejudice against the more progressive candidate. It is only fair to add that Emily Davies' brother, Llewelyn Davies, was later Principal of Queen's.

No wonder that in 1866 Emily Davies came to the conclusion that the only way to secure an equal education for young women was to found a new college, attached to a university where there was sympathy in some quarters, and where the intellectual standards would be rigorously enforced. Girton was the answer; founded at Hitchin in 1869 and moved to Girton village on the outskirts of Cambridge in 1873.[1]

The contribution of Queen's to the expansion of educational opportunities for girls was to educate so many pioneers in the

[1] See M. C. Bradbrook, *'That Infidel Place'. A Short History of Girton College. 1869—1969* (1969).

field, while the College itself remained on the fringe of the movement. The *Englishwoman's Journal*, the *Victoria Magazine* (to which Maurice was an occasional contributor), the women's suffrage campaign, the Social Science Association and the pressure to allow women to sit for university examinations were all initiated and encouraged by a small circle of women who had connections with Queen's. Barbara Leigh Smith, later Madame Bodichon, attended a few lectures at Queen's; she was a niece of Julia Smith and cousin of Florence Nightingale. Later she campaigned for the Married Women's Property Act and became a friend of George Eliot.

Dorothea Beale was a student and then a tutor at Queen's. She was always grateful to Queen's for the sympathy and intellectual stimulation she received. To a lesser extent this was true of her contemporary, Frances Mary Buss. Each went on to become a great headmistress. In their intellectual standards, they owed much to Queen's; in other ways, Queen's served as no useful model for them, and their own schools were not copies of the College. Three younger pupils also became great headmistresses. Alice Bishop (a student 1858–63) who became a headmistress of two of the schools belonging to the Girls' Public Day School Company; her sister, Matilda Bishop (a student 1858–60) who was headmistress of Kensington High School and then the first Principal of the Royal Holloway College; and Frances Dove (student 1860–2) who was the second headmistress of St Leonard's School, St Andrews, before founding Wycombe Abbey School.

The story of the opening of the medical profession to women is linked with the history of Queen's.[1] Sophia Jex-Blake was first a student (1858) and then a tutor (1859–61) at Queen's before a visit to America and a meeting with some women doctors fired her with the ambition to study medicine. She and four other young women more or less forced their way into Edinburgh University; masculine prejudice thwarted their first efforts, but they eventually qualified at Dublin University, and Sophia Jex-

[1] The full story can be read in E. Moberley Bell, *Storming the Citadel* (1953).

Blake helped to found the London School of Medicine for Women. Emily Bovell (student 1855–60) also began studying at Edinburgh but completed her course in Paris, where she took the M.D. degree in 1877. She was later appointed physician at the new hospital for women in Marylebone Road, and at the same time came into Queen's to give lectures in physiology and hygiene. Helen Prideaux (1869–73) was a brilliant medical student; she gained a gold medal and exhibition for Anatomy at London University, but died at the age of thirty before establishing the reputation which would undoubtedly have been hers had she survived. A later student still, Eleanor Davies-Colley, was the first woman to be elected a Fellow of the Royal College of Surgeons.

G. M. Young reminds us that during the nineteenth century, women 'were becoming an effective element in the articulation of the social mind'.[1] Many Queen's students left to take up some form of social work. One of the most effective and articulate was Louisa Twining, one of the earliest students. Her chief work was the improvement of conditions in workhouses; in achieving this, she was one of the first women to be elected to a Board of Guardians. She also found time to write books on mediaeval art.

If Queen's could produce such pioneers, why did it 'grow Conservative', and yield no response to the suggestions of people like Miles Beale and Emily Davies? Would it have done so if Maurice had remained Chairman of the Committee of Education?

Maurice was a cautious reformer. In 1855, he poured scorn on the movement for opening the professions to women, and for admitting them to degrees.[2] But by the 1860s, he was giving a modified support to Emily Davies. When he moved to Cambridge in 1866, his lectures were attended by mixed audiences, with almost as many women as men. In 1870, he was involved in the lectures which formed the basis of Newnham College. He was

[1] In *Victorian England: Portrait of an Age* (1936).

[2] See his lecture on *The Plan of a Female College for the help of the rich and the poor,* delivered in May 1855 and published in *Lectures to Ladies on practical subjects* (1855).

more flexible in his outlook and more deeply sympathetic to the cause of women's education than many of his successors.

Maurice's successor as Chairman and as Principal was Richard Trench; Trench's successor was Arthur Stanley. Trench was a scholar and a churchman. While holding the Principalship of Queen's, he was a Professor at King's, and after 1856, the Dean of Westminster. Though an admirer and friend of Maurice throughout his life, he was no socialist, and had neither the time nor the inclination to become involved in the emancipation movement.[1] Stanley, Trench's successor at both Westminster and Queen's, was an even more remote figure, and made infrequent and irregular visits to the College. The administration of the College was left largely to the genial Plumptre, another scholar–clergyman. He was a respected teacher and a good disciplinarian, but not a reformer or innovator. These were not the men to become the architects of a social revolution. They were basically conservative, and fully involved in many other responsibilities.

Dorothea Beale wrote in the Jubilee Book:

> I have always regretted that my *Alma Mater*, which should have held the first rank, as it was the first in time, has not done so, owing to some faults—I venture to think in its first constitution.

This was true. The constitution divided the responsibility for the College between the Committee of Education and the Council in a most unsatisfactory way so that neither had real initiative. With the Lady Visitors poised between them, the scene was set for strife. The Council consisted largely of absentee clerics and peers, with the caustic Edmund Becket Denison as Chairman.[2]

[1] Though he helped Mrs Anne Jellicoe to found Alexandra College, on the model of Queen's in Dublin in 1866.

[2] In 1866, the Council members were R. C. Trench (Archbishop of Dublin), John Lonsdale (Bishop of Lichfield), Samuel Wilberforce (Bishop of Oxford), Lord Ebury, Lord Richard Cavendish, Sir Walter James, H. Alford (Dean of Canterbury), Rev R. W. Browne,

After Maurice, no influential member of the College staff or Council was able to provide adventurous leadership. Llewelyn Davies made an attempt, but was finally frustrated.

This was partly because the membership was still entirely male. If one thinks of the opening of Girton College, the founding of the School of Medicine for Women, the opening of degrees to women, the impetus came primarily from women, encouraged and helped by men, it is true. Queen's had now no visionary to point the way forward.

Rev H. W. Burrows, Rev F. C. Cook, E. B. Denison, Rev C. J. D'Oyly, A. J. Beresford Hope, Dr George Johnson, Rev James Lonsdale, Rev J. R. Major, A. P. Stanley (Dean of Westminster).

VIII

The Schools' Inquiry Commission 1868

It is now worth taking stock of the position of Queen's in the year the Schools' Inquiry Commission Report was published—1868. The College was twenty-years-old and well established. It was now possible to evaluate some of its achievements, its status and its promise.

In 1864 the Government appointed a commission to deal with the schools not already dealt with by the Newcastle Commission on elementary education in 1861 or the Clarendon Commission on public schools in 1864. The Assistant Commissioners were told:

> You will understand that you are required to give your chief attention to the schools attended by the children of such of the gentry, clergy, professional and commercial men as are of limited means, and of farmers and of tradesmen.

Emily Davies wrote to Matthew Arnold to ask whether girls' schools were to be included in the survey. He replied:

> I can hardly think that the new Commission, with all it will have on its hands, will be willing to undertake the enquiry into girls' schools as well as that into boys'.[1]

This was the signal for action. Emily Davies and Eliza Bostock, a friend of Mrs Reid and a Council member of Bedford College, drew up a memorial to the Commissioners. Several people connected with Queen's and Bedford signed it; amongst

[1] Quoted in Barbara Stephen, *Emily Davies and Girton College* (1927), pp. 130–1.

them were Maurice, Dean Stanley, Plumptre and many of the Lady Visitors. The suggestion was accepted and Mr Roby, secretary to the Commissioners, actually offered to help. He did in fact co-operate in the most friendly way, allowing Emily Davies to comment on the questions and instructions to be sent to the Assistant Commissioners. She also suggested that J. S. Mill, Mark Pattison and T. H. Huxley should be included amongst the witnesses summoned before the Commission. Both she and Dorothea Beale were later summoned as witnesses.

The commissioner appointed to examine girls' schools in London was D. R. Fearon. He visited Queen's in 1865, three years before the Report was actually published. His findings can be read in Volume VII.

In the introduction, he stated that there were only four public girls' schools in London which provided education for students up to the age of eighteen. They were Queen's, Bedford, the Clergy Orphan School and the Adult Orphan Institution. Of these, Queen's and Bedford were singled out:

> These two colleges represent the first, and almost, indeed, the only attempts which have been made in London to establish girls' education of the first grade upon a thoroughly public basis, in colleges offering guarantees for the soundness of the education similar in kind to those offered by public schools for boys, though without sacrificing that retirement and unobtrusiveness which are considered essential for the preservation of the freshness and refinement of female character.

He commented on the comparative social exclusiveness of the students:

> The pupils who attend these colleges belong principally to the upper middle class. They are chiefly daughters of professional men, such as clergymen, lawyers, doctors, teachers, artists and the like. There is, however, among them a certain number, of the daughters of tradesmen, clerks and others engaged in mercantile pursuits. There is

> also a certain number, especially at Queen's College, of the daughters of the upper classes. Considerable care is exercised in the admission of pupils, and the daughters of persons keeping public-houses are, I believe, excluded from both colleges. The fact, however, that the colleges are only used for instruction, and not for boarding, renders a greater mixture of classes possible than would otherwise be advisable.

It has always been possible for a few students to come to Queen's without paying fees, by winning scholarships. In 1865 there were altogether 26 pupils for whom no fees were paid; some were the children of professors, some were nominated by the G.B.I. and the others were holders of the nine available scholarships.

Mr Fearon's general conclusion about the first grade of girls' schools was that the provision was wholly inadequate; there were not enough schools, the buildings were unsatisfactory, there was a lack of educated women teachers, and the costs were high. He remarked, for example, that whereas it would not cost more than £9 a year to send a boy to the City of London School, it would cost at least £28. 10. 0 to send a girl of fifteen to Queen's (Music and Drawing cost extra). But, as Emily Davies would have been the first to point out, so many boys' schools had inherited endowments, many of which had originally been given for 'children', and not necessarily specifically for boys. No-one had thought of appropriating them for girls.

The Commission found much to criticise in boys' schools as well as the girls' schools. But their problems and shortcomings were not the same.

The report on Queen's is printed in the Appendix and takes up fourteen pages. It gives a detailed description of the College, with comments at the end and suggestions for improvement. First of all, we have the opportunity to see the College as it appeared to a sympathetic outside observer. The College was a day school, though the Council and committee had given approval to ladies to receive pupils in their own houses.

The staff list shows several changes from the original one, with only four who had been in the College since the beginning:

Arithmetic, Geometry and Algebra	Mr Cock
Drawing and Pictorial Art	Mr W. Cave Thomas Mr A. Warren
Landscape Drawing	Mr H. Warren—Mr A. Warren
English Language and Literature	Mr Maurice[1]—Mr Benham
French	Mr Mariette
Geography	Mr Hughes
German	Dr Weil
Harmony	Mr Hullah—Mr Bannister
History, Ancient	Mr Plumptre
History, Modern	Mr Maurice—Mr Benham
Italian	Mr Biaggi
Latin	Mr Meyrick
Musical Composition	Dr Sterndale Bennett
Natural Philosophy and Astronomy	Mr Cock
Philosophy—mental and moral	Mr Garden
Theology and Church History	Mr Cheetham—Mr Garden (occasional lectures by Dr Stanley)
Vocal Music	Mr Hullah—Mr May Mr Bannister—Mr Hopkins
Writing	Mr Goldsmith

This shows no substantial change from the subjects offered in 1848. There had been a suggestion that Rhetoric might be introduced, but Mrs Denison wrote to Plumptre that her husband (one of the most active Council members) 'begs me to say that he does not see any good in teaching young ladies Rhetoric, as they are generally supposed to talk quite enough without learning it'.

Apart from the professors, there was also a list of 'teachers appointed for the assistance of pupils requiring additional

[1] In 1866 (soon after this list was compiled). Maurice was appointed Knightbridge Professor of Casuistry, Moral Theology and Moral Philosophy at Cambridge, and resigned his position at Queen's. His successor as Professor of History at Queen's was John Richard Green.

instruction', a list of eleven women. All these, except Mademoiselle Rosin de Pratz, who taught French conversation, were former students. Two of them later gained distinction in their own spheres; Rosa Morrison became the Lady Superintendent of women students at University College, and Emily Bovell became a distinguished physician.

The status of these women, who were being paid as teachers, was often equivocal, and the idea of girls from good families taking on such a position was sometimes criticised. Sophia Jex-Blake had been a tutor at Queen's between 1859 and 1861. Her father had written to her on hearing this information:

> Dearest, I have only this moment heard that you contemplate being *paid* for the tutorship. It would be quite beneath you, darling, and I *cannot consent* to it. Take the post as one of honour and usefulness, and I shall be glad, and *you will be no loser,* be quite sure. But to be *paid* for the work would be to alter the thing *completely,* and would lower you sadly in the eyes of almost everybody. Do not think about it, dearest, and you will rejoice greatly, by and bye, with all who love you best.[1]

She eventually resisted her father's pleadings, and took the salary.

The syllabus laid down by the Committee of Education offered a substantial diet:

Subjects	*1st Junior*	*2nd Junior*	*1st and 2nd Senior*
Arithmetic, Geometry, and Algebra	The Four Compound Rules—Rule of Three. Vulgar Fractions—Fractions	Vulgar Fractions—Double Rule of Three. Percentage and Interest—Principles of Geometry—Euclid's B.I.	Decimal Fractions—Square and Cube Root. Miscellaneous Questions—Euclid's Elements, I, II, III—Algebra

[1] See Margaret Todd, *Life of Sophia Jex-Blake* (1918).

THE SCHOOLS' INQUIRY COMMISSION

Subjects	*1st Junior*	*2nd Junior*	*1st and 2nd Senior*
Astronomy			Herschel's Outlines
Drawing	Elementary Drawing from the Round	Drawing from the Round	Figure from the Antique—Landscape from Models
English	Grammar—Analysis of Sentences—Morell's English Grammar—Reading	Composition and History of Language—Reading. Bacon's Essays. Milton's Minor Poems	Literature—The seventeenth and eighteenth centuries
French	Grammar—Reading—Conservation—Brasseur's Grammar and Manual	Translation—Idioms—Etymology—Racine Mariette's Half Hours	Idioms—Composition—La Fontaine—Literature and History
Geography	Elementary—Hughes' Modern Geography	Physical—Guyot's Earth and Man	Historical—Progress of Discovery and Commerce. The Bristol Colonies. Hughes' Manual of Geography
German	Elements of Grammar. Oetrogge's Deutsches Lesebuch, 1st Course	Grammar—Exercises. Schiller's Thirty Years' War	Exercises—Schiller's Wilhelm Tell—Goethe's Hermann und Dorothea. Wilmar's Literatur-geschichte
Harmony			Counterpoint—Composition
History, Ancient	Biblical—Early Greek	Greek—Roman	Biblical—Oriental
History, Modern	The Kings of England (Mosley's)	Early English	English—The seventeenth and eighteenth centuries. Modern—From the fourteenth to the eighteenth century

Subjects	*1st Junior*	*2nd Junior*	*1st and 2nd Senior*
Italian		Grammar—Biaggi's Prosatori	Tasso—Manzoni—Dante—Composition History of Literature
Latin	London Latin Grammar. Adam's Selectae Sententiae	Henry's First Latin Book. Cornelius Nepos	Composition—Virgil—Cicero
Philosophy, Natural	Lardner's School Course		Lardner's Course—Ganot's Cours de Physique
Philosophy, Mental and Moral			Butler's Three Sermons—Hooker, Book I
Theology	Gospel according to St Matthew—The Creed. Robertson's Sketches of Church History	The Acts of the Apostles—Old Testament	The book of Psalms—Church History—The Reformation
Vocal Music	Theory and Practice of Singing at Sight	Theory and Practice of Singing at sight	Practice of Choral and Concerted Music

Mr Fearon praised the lectures given in the College. He attended several himself; 'they all seemed to be instructive, and some of them to be brilliant'. Then came his criticism:

> Considering the inequality of age in the pupils, and considering also the extremely imperfect and unequal condition of their knowledge and attainments when they enter, considering also the apathy and indifference prevalent among girls respecting the subjects of solid, as opposed to ornamental instruction, I would venture to suggest whether the mode of instruction carried on in this college is sufficiently tutorial; whether it is not too exclusively professorial, conducted rather by means of the delivery of lectures than by requiring sound and systematic work from the pupils. Unless I am greatly mistaken the majority of

> these pupils are not fit for lectures, but are in great need of close and strict schooling.

The Committee promised to take note of his criticism, but it is not clear that any definite change of policy was made. Lectures continued to be the means of education; those who were able to benefit from them did so, and the rest were left to flounder or dream or muddle through. At any rate, the lectures were tolerated by those who were ill-prepared, and Mr Fearon found the atmosphere of the College to be 'simple, quiet, orderly and free from all excitement'.

The second main criticism led to more positive action. It concerned the question of certificates given to the students. We remember that the College was actually started for the purpose of granting certificates to governesses, as a guarantee of standard for their prospective employers. The granting of these certificates had continued to play an important part in the College's work, and there were people who took certificates without having attended any lectures. For example, Jessie Boucherett started a school in Charlotte Street for shop assistants. She took twenty pupils, gave them tuition in English, Arithmetic and Bookkeeping and then had them examined at the end of term by teachers at Queen's.

There was an outline syllabus for these examinations. For example, in English Language and Literature, it was the following:

Third Class—Morell's Grammar and Analysis of Sentences. Shakespeare's Julius Caesar, ed. Craik.

Second Class—(Additional) History of Language. Milton's Minor Poems. Bacon's Advancement of Learning, Book I.

First Class—(Additional) History of Literature of 17th century. Spenser's Faery Queen. Book I.

Books recommended—Hallam: History of Literature Latham: Handbook of English Language. Craik: History of English Language.

The examiners for all these subjects were the professors of the College. It was possible to take a certificate in a particular subject, or to take a 'certificate of proficiency', by presenting oneself for examination in up to three subjects. It was this certificate which Mr Fearon particularly criticised, as not living up to its name.

We have already seen that both Miles Beale and Emily Davies wanted Queen's to lead the way in finding a more objective assessment of the standard reached by girls. They wanted some recognition from the universities. What was wholly commendable in 1848—teaching and examination by the same professors—was no longer acceptable in 1868. Mr Fearon took the same line:

> It may now . . . be a question whether, considering the length of time the college has been established, and the greater familiarity with examinations which the action of Cambridge University, and other bodies, had introduced among women, the time is not arrived for Queen's College to take a higher line. The principle of issuing certificates, whether of special or general proficiency, on the result of examinations, conducted by the teachers who have been instructing the candidates in these subjects, is an essentially unsound principle.

In fact, this was his chief criticism of all the education for girls which he saw:

> What is wanted is an uniform, public, authoritative, and (above all) entirely independent test of knowledge, similar to the examinations of Oxford and Cambridge, or such as might be provided by the opening of the examinations of the London University to women . . . This matter seems to lie at the root of all improvements in the education of girls, and is the point which I desire most strongly to impress on the Commissioners.

The Committee of Education had been notoriously sluggish

and conservative on this point. It is hard to see why; surely they had no reason to fear the consequences. They now took this criticism more seriously, and appointed a sub-committee to investigate; it reported at length. The Committee then agreed to the appointment of special outside examiners, who were to start their work in 1869. Yet in 1871, we find the Committee of Education voting, by a majority of 4 to 2, in favour of the motion 'that the examination by the professors themselves is better suited to the circumstances of the College'. It was not without a struggle that the professors gave up their exclusive control.

The Committee revised the Certificate of Proficiency, and substituted a Certificate of Associateship. Candidates for this could qualify by attendance at the College for six terms, and by gaining an average mark of at least 66% in five subjects. Eminent past pupils were eligible for a sort of honorary associateship.

This certificate still exists. It was a forerunner of matriculation, with a similar balance of subjects; one science, English, and another language, for example, being compulsory. It was a more sensible and balanced certificate than the previous one, but it still did not provide the outsider with an objective standard.

At the time when the Schools' Inquiry Commission was investigating and reporting on the condition of Queen's, the Principal and Chairman of the Committee of Education was Dean Stanley. He had succeeded Richard Trench as Dean of Westminster, and succeeded him at Queen's as well. He accepted the position in February 1864, and a few months later sent a message to say that he would only be able to give four or five lectures on consecutive days each term. From this time until 1871, when the Committee of Education became concerned that he ought to take 'a larger share in the general management of the college', he never once attended its meetings, though he was the chairman. He gave a few lectures, but appointed a deputy to deliver most of the Church History lectures. The following year he resigned. It seems to have been a genuine misunderstanding. He did not have the same feeling of adventure and novelty as the earlier pioneers. Yet adventurous leadership was what the College most needed.

The work of administration devolved upon the Dean, Edward Plumptre. Plumptre was Maurice's brother-in-law. He was a scholar, having taken a traditional double first at Oxford in Classics and Mathematics, and but for his marriage might have devoted his life to scholarship in Oxford as a Fellow of Brasenose College. But his marriage to Harriet Maurice disqualified him and he came to London to join the staff of King's. Here he stayed for thirty-four years until he was appointed Dean of Wells. At King's he was not only Professor of Pastoral Theology and Exegesis, but he gave his services as dean of the evening classes which started in the 1850s. He joined the Committee of Education at Queen's at the beginning in 1848, and was soon taking Greek classes. For the first year, the Greek class consisted of Dorothea Beale and a friend, and it remained one of Dorothea Beale's happiest recollections of Queen's. She was so keen that she remembered working at Homer on the day of the Duke of Wellington's funeral, while her friends took a holiday. After four terms the class was closed for lack of support, and Dorothea mourned the fact that her brother's tutor at home, to whom she now resorted, was not nearly so inspiring a teacher. Later, Plumptre taught Ancient History and Latin. It was said that he used to work out his translations of Dante on his walk from Kensington to Queen's across the parks.

Plumptre was popular, though strict. Camilla Croudace remembered him thus:

> In appearance he had a very Roman face. I have seen in Roman galleries many ancient Romans like him. Especially do I remember a bust still standing in one of the courts at Pompeii. His manner was shy, but, at the same time, very genial and kind; however, he certainly inspired a wholesome awe, and it was a very serious thing to be reported to the Dean.

Here is a letter from a pupil who was reported to the Dean:

> It is with great feelings of respect, and regret, that I thus presume to address you; in order to offer you my most sincere apologies, for having so far forgotten myself as a lady, as to have had any part in throwing the parcel; had I but

> reflected for one moment I should have foreseen the trouble, and anxiety it would have given both you, and Mrs Williams, and the stigma of it would have cast upon myself: I feel that no apology on my part can be sufficient to you, but I trust by my future conduct, and progress, to prove to you the sincerity of my regret. I hope you will believe how much I thank you for your impressive and gentle rebuke, which I can never forget.

And here is a letter which Plumptre wrote in 1864 to Miss Elizabeth Twining as representative of the Lady Visitors, showing how circumspect he was and had to be in his dealing with them:

> A suggestion has been made that I should permit the girls to act a charade or two at the festival *without any change of dress*. The objections of the Lady Visitors and the Council, if I understand them rightly, were chiefly directed against the *costume* of performance and the theatrical display which it involved, and I should therefore be glad to know whether you think I might sanction such a performance as I have described without coming into collision with the feelings of the Visitors . . .

The charade was not performed.

Plumptre was Dean for nineteen years, and finally served as Principal for four. He set scholarly standards, gave loyal service to the College and set a good tone. He wanted to share the delights of learning with his pupils, but would not share in the aspirations of Emily Davies and her friends. From this controversy he preferred to remain aloof.

Queen's was a day school but there were always a few girls who lived too far away for them to travel each day, and there seemed to be a steady application from middle-aged ladies who wanted to earn a little money by taking in a few students. By 1866, both Miss Parry and Mrs Boole, the Librarian, were taking students in residence on the premises. The Council and Committee of Education 'licensed' these people, so to speak, but otherwise each lady concerned ran her residence as a private venture.

Mrs Boole[1] was a remarkable and eccentric character who was eventually regarded with some suspicion by the College staff. Her husband was George Boole, an unconventional mathematician whose originality and ability are only now being fully recognised. Both husband and wife were admirers of F. D. Maurice, and when George Boole died, Mary Boole applied for help to Maurice. Maurice was probably responsible for her being given the post of Librarian at Queen's in 1865, and for her being given the tenancy of the upper part of no 68. She ran a boarding house there for students until 1873, while her own daughters also attended the College. She had wide-ranging interests, including psychology, psychic science and Judaism, as well as mathematics, and held 'true logic' classes on Sunday evenings, when she encouraged students to bring their problems to be discussed. No doubt she gave the students under her care considerable intellectual stimulation. But she was also an unstable character, and it was probably a combination of instability and 'dangerous' ideas which led the Committee of Education to terminate her lease of part of the premises in 1873.

There is one more aspect to Queen's to mention—the building. In education, the most important influence is personality and character; nothing will make up for lack of good teachers. Environment comes second, but it is important. The Schools' Inquiry Commissioners regarded Queen's as 'neither better nor worse provided than most of the educational institutions for girls in London'. It was quite fair to point out that the College occupied houses originally built for private residence; that the street outside was noisy and sometimes the lessons were interrupted; and that there was no proper playground. These criticisms would still hold. But we should also take into consideration the quality of the buildings. This particular block of houses in Harley Street, between Queen Anne Street and New Cavendish Street, was built in 1762. The style is Georgian. Outside, the design is simple and well-proportioned. Inside there is more decoration—

[1] See Eleanor Cobham, *Mary Everest Boole* (1951).

moulded ceilings and an elegant staircase—and there are several beautifully proportioned rooms.

The present 45 Harley Street was the first house of the College, while no 43 was acquired eight years later. No 47 remained the headquarters of the G.B.I. until the present century. The centre of the College was the Waiting Room, behind the staircase of no 45; here the pupils were collected by their parents or governesses. Near-by was the Library, which used to have a fire in the winter. The Waiting Room is still used as a preparation room, but the Library has expanded and moved upstairs, and with it the portrait of Maurice by Lowes Dickinson.

Most of the classrooms were upstairs. An exception was 'Mr Cock's room', the present Chemistry laboratory. Lady Tree wrote of the different ways of reaching it in the Jubilee Book:

> There were three ways of getting to it. One way was by the door—the right way. Another and a better way was after a Descensus Averni of cellars and underground passages, to emerge from the floor of the room through a trap door. The third and the best was by the window—one reached it through the dressing room skylight, a tiresome effort. Thence across the leads to a drop of some twenty feet, which, with luck, landed one in time to be discovered meekly elucidating Euclid, dolorously digging for square roots, or groping in darkness for the truth about light.

Unfortunately changes to the structure of the building have reduced the possible ways of reaching the laboratory to the first one only.

Altogether it was and is a building to which one could become very much attached—a building of character. This was already true of both building and institution by 1868.

IX

1872–86. Development or Decline?

ON the day after Easter Sunday 1872, Frederick Denison Maurice died in Cambridge. After retiring from Queen's on his removal to Cambridge, he had not lost interest in furthering the opportunities for education for girls. In 1870 he had written to Plumptre:

> There is an endowment fund beginning in connexion with our Cambridge classes for women. Mill and his step-daughter have contributed £40 for two years to it. I suppose they are influenced partly by Mrs Fawcett's presence on our Committee; but it is a proof that he does not spend all his zeal for women's emancipation in discourse. I think the endowment will be bestowed on girls who have passed the Local Examination very well and who wish to avail themselves of our Lectures. There is some prospect of a sister of Mrs G. Butler, Mrs Masson, settling here for the purpose of receiving pupils into her house. The Lectures have only lasted a term and as yet we are only beginning to catch any besides wives and daughters of the University; but there is a sprinkling from the shops and we hope to increase it.[1]

In 1870 he wrote a letter to the *Spectator* supporting the idea of female suffrage; a correspondence with John Stuart Mill followed, but Mill was unable to persuade him to talk at a public meeting on the subject.

His was the greatest intellect and the greatest character connected with Queen's. Gladstone, one of his great contemporaries, found him puzzling, as do many today who try to

[1] MS letter in the possession of Queen's College. The lectures referred to were the beginning of Newnham College.

read his theology. Some years after Maurice's death, Gladstone wrote:

> Maurice is indeed a spiritual splendour, to borrow a phrase of Dante about St Dominic. His intellectual constitution had long been, and still is, to me a good deal of an enigma. When I remember what is said and thought of him, and by whom, I feel that this must be greatly my own fault.[1]

It is that enigma which still fascinates us today.

At the time of Maurice's death, the Committee of Education began searching for a new Principal to replace Dean Stanley. Dean Church refused, Canon Barry of King's felt he could not take on additional work, and Plumptre, though sympathetic, was not prepared to reside permanently in London. After further searching, the Committee asked the Bishop, as Visitor, to nominate the Rev J. Llewelyn Davies; he became Principal in 1873.

John Llewelyn Davies can best be described first as the brother of Emily Davies, founder of Girton College. This means that during the previous decade he had known all about and supported his sister's attempts to open university examinations to women, to extend the franchise to women, and to appropriate school endowments for the education of girls. He also supported her successful attempt to establish a college for women at Hitchin to prepare them to take the degree examinations at Cambridge—later Girton College. This was one excellent qualification for association with Queen's.

Another qualification for his association with Queen's was his admiration for Maurice. Llewelyn Davies was educated at Repton and Trinity College, Cambridge. At Cambridge he distinguished himself by being elected President of the Union, and by being placed fifth in the classical tripos. For a year he was a Fellow of Trinity, worked on a translation of Plato's *Republic* and taught, among others, Leslie Stephen.

It was at Cambridge that he first came under the influence of Maurice. A leading bookseller was Daniel Macmillan who had

[1] Morley, *Life of Gladstone*, vol. I (1903), pp. 454–5.

recently launched out into publishing. His friends and patrons included Maurice, Kingsley and Trench, and it was their books he published; pre-eminently Maurice's *Theological Essays*. Through Macmillan's influence, Davies became interested in Maurice, and later in life was able to expound and clarify many of Maurice's ideas which others found difficult to follow.

In 1881 he was ordained and moved to London, where for thirty-seven years he was a parish priest, most of the time at Christ Church, Lisson Grove, described by a contemporary as 'an unfragrant neighbourhood near the Edgware Road station of the Metropolitan Railway'. His form of escape was walking and climbing and he was an original member of the Alpine Club.

Llewelyn Davies was regarded as a typical Broad Churchman. Broad Churchmanship has been recently described as the 'identification of Church and State to the closest possible degree. . . . In the realization of some such ideal the Broad Church school saw the solution to many, if not all, the political and social problems racking England in the nineteenth century.'[1] It was in this spirit that Davies had first suggested the compromise of unsectarian religious teaching in the Board schools to be set up under the Education Act of 1871—the Cowper–Temple clause. He was a follower of Maurice in believing that practice should support precept. He helped the Christian Socialists with the co-operative workshops and taught at the Working Men's College. Later he was an active member of the London School Board and supported the legalisation of Trade Unions.

Emily Davies had already attempted, unsuccessfully, to affiliate Queen's to Cambridge so that students might take degrees. The failure led to the new venture at Hitchin. Now her brother had plans to enable students at Queen's to take the examinations and if possible the degrees of London University. He prepared a memorandum to this effect and had it circulated to the members of the Committee of Education. Emily Davies meanwhile wrote to Madame Bodichon early in 1874:

[1] Article by R. T. Shannon on *J. R. Seeley and the Idea of a National Church* in *Ideas and Institutions of Victorian Britain*, ed. R. Robson (1967).

> There is a prospect of reform at Queen's College. My brother has been made Principal, and he is aiming at getting it reconstituted on the model of University and King's, i.e. having a good *school* for girls under 18, and making them pass an Entrance Examination for admission to the College; which might then be a place of advanced teaching, preparing for London University Examinations.

The Committee hedged its responsibility for discussing this memorandum seriously, and a valid excuse was found when the premises needed extensive repair and the College had to move for six months to 3 Stratford Place. Once again the opportunity for fruitful development was lost. But one thing the committee did agree to was that admission to the College should be by examination, not just by age.

Another representation came from the Lady Visitors, who complained of 'the steady decrease in the number of Compounding Pupils', and suggested that one cause might be 'the total absence of women's influence in the Government of a College expressly intended for the education of women.' The Committee showed sympathy with this request, and agreed to elect six Lady Visitors to their number each year. The first six to be elected were Lady Stanley of Alderley, Lady Monteagle, Mrs Wollaston Blake, Mrs Hensleigh Wedgwood, Mrs Theodore Williams and Miss Anna Swanwick.

Unfortunately at the same meeting as this was agreed, Llewelyn Davies handed in his resignation, because he was not satisfied with the existing organisation of the College, particularly with the division of responsibility between the Council and the Committee of Education. In his place, Plumptre was appointed Principal and remained such for the next three years.

Plumptre took over a College whose numbers were declining and whose government and discipline were subject to criticism. One of the people he consulted was his niece by marriage, Emily Hill,[1] who had been a student for two years between 1858 and

[1] Sister of Octavia Hill. Octavia took two Latin certificates at Queen's, in 1863 and 1864, but there is no record in the College archives of her ever having been a student.

1860; she was now married to Maurice's son, Charles Edmund Maurice, Lecturer, in Modern History at Queen's. This is what she wrote to him:

> I know that persons in authority sometimes are deep in ignorance of facts which would be very helpful to them, just because no one likes to put before them disagreeable truths, and this must be my excuse for troubling you with this letter.
>
> (1) The Lady Visitors in my time were so irregular in their attendance that they were *no* guarantee for the order of the classes. Edmund has only had a Lady Visitor at his class about three times.
>
> (2) They much more often went to the lectures, than to the language or mathematical classes, and as in the two latter the personal intercourse between professor and pupil is much greater, there is much more need of supervision.
>
> (3) I have heard from several sources that the want of more definite supervision is felt to be a great drawback to the working of the College, and that many parents are deterred from sending their girls on that account. And if the more carefully brought up girls are withdrawn, of course the general tone of the College must be lowered.
>
> It seems to me that if the system of Lady Visitors is to be worth anything, each lady should hold herself responsible for being present at some particular class, and if prevented from attending should give the Lady Superintendent due notice; so that a substitute might be found, and no class *ever* left without the presence of a lady.
>
> (4) With regard to the Mathematical classes, I know that very little real work is done in them.
>
> (5) I believe that all the pupils who care most for the College have desired for it above everything the influence of some really noble woman. They think that the Lady Superintendent ought to be the soul of the College and therefore a person of sufficient character to be more independent of the Ladies' Committee and Council; a woman of first rate powers and above all with a lofty ideal before her; so that

> she should be able to keep the tone right among the girls, enter with true sympathy into all their intellectual pursuits, be a link between them and their teachers, and above all make herself respected by professors, Lady Visitors, parents and Council; so that she should not be a mere tool in their hands; but a bond between them all, putting life into the whole machinery of the College.[1]

By this time, the first schools of the Girls' Public Day School Company had been founded, and Cheltenham and North London Collegiate School were well established—all with women staff. These staff were in many cases former students of Queen's; very few had taken a full university course. Queen's was beginning to admit more women to the staff, but not until 1888 was a woman nominated for a Professorship; Agnata Ramsay, the only candidate to be placed in the first division of the first class of the classical tripos in 1887, was nominated as Professor of Greek, but withdrew her name.

Most of the women on the staff either taught in the school, or gave private lessons on the piano. Miss M. A. Parry was the person of longest standing in 1875. She had devoted most of her working life to Queen's, and Queen's in its turn had given her an education and status she might not have found elsewhere. Her father had failed in business when she was twelve, and she had first taught her younger sister and brother, and then become a governess when she was nineteen, serving three families in turn. As soon as Queen's opened, she attended the evening classes, and was very soon engaged as the first Superintendent of the School. After eight years, she became the Lady Resident and held the position for twenty-two years. Though a great supporter of the expansion of opportunities of education for women, she refused to sign the petition asking for Cambridge examinations to be open to women, because she so much disapproved of competition.

The Lady Visitors petitioned Plumptre to appoint a new Lady Resident on the grounds that Miss Parry

[1] MS letter in the possession of Queen's College.

> has not exercised that influence for good over the character and general culture of our pupils which ought, we venture to think, to form one of the first duties of her office.

Though Miss Parry had been there a long time and was elderly, one cannot help thinking that the Lady Visitors, and Mrs C. E. Maurice, expected a lot. Plumptre, who was kind-hearted, did not agree with their verdict on Miss Parry, but he was out-voted in the Committee of Education, who offered Miss Parry a pension of £100 a year and advertised her post. She spent the next four years helping in a school for small boys in Eastbourne, then finally retired and lived until 1896.

Her successor was Miss Eleanor Grove, already the assistant secretary. Miss Grove was a resolute and determined feminist, who roused the ire of the chairman of the Council on more than one occasion. She was first appointed in 1872, having been chosen from forty-five applicants without even appearing at the interview because a telegram to Vienna was delayed. Evidently she was a nominee of Lord Ebury, who made a rare appearance at a Council meeting to vote her in. Nine days later Becket Denison (chairman of the Council) wrote to Plumptre:

> I am sorry to hear our entries seriously decline from competition. I wonder whether your new strong-minded female-suffrage under-secretary will be able to revive them. I hear we have incurred some obloquy by electing an invisible woman. But when Lords previously invisible through any telescope come to job a person in it is no use to suggest postponement. I daresay she is a capital woman, but a more barefaced job than his appearance I have never seen, even from a sanctimonious nobleman.

Two years later, Denison threatened to resign if this 'energetic secretary' continued to interfere and lead a 'reform party'. (It was a very great pity when Denison[1] did retire in 1878, because his letters and comments were always good value.)

[1] Later Sir Edmund Becket, then Lord Grimthorpe. See Peter Ferriday, *Lord Grimthorpe* (1957).

When Eleanor Grove was appointed Lady Resident, she set to work in earnest. Her duties were to maintain order in the Waiting Room and the library, to keep the register, to superintend the College servants and to give general guidance to the pupils in their studies. Within a month or two she had sent Plumptre a list of complaints, particularly about the Lady Visitors; there were 84 classes a week, and the maximum number of classes visited in one week by the Lady Visitors was 13. Their attendance improved after this complaint, though not their liking for Miss Grove.

Miss Grove's friend was Rosa Morison, who was tutor in German, Italian and Latin for fifteen years. Both of them despaired of the procrastination of the Committee in doing anything about the inefficient and ineffective teaching given by a minority of the professors. They resigned in 1881 and went on to other spheres. Miss Grove's successor was Camilla Croudace, a former student and a remarkable woman who for almost three decades influenced the life of the College with her personality and character. She was at last the 'woman of first rate powers' whom Mrs Maurice wanted the College to find.

Two other women played a significant part in the life of the School. There was Miss Hay, who was the Superintendent for over thirty years, from 1862 until 1893, and Rosalind Hosking, who was in charge of the kindergarten for fifteen years, and ran it according to Pestalozzi's ideas.

In the College, Mademoiselle Séguin was employed as a tutor in 1879 and Miss Kilgour in 1880. Both stayed for at least twenty-five years, and we shall have more to say of them later. Most of the government and teaching of the College remained in the hands of men, and Queen's remained persistently different from the girls' schools now springing up all over the country. One reason for this, of course, was that Queen's was neither a school nor a college. It was not until the present century that it became clearly an educational institution of pre-university standard. (In retaining men on its staff, it has now, in the nineteen seventies, found itself fully up to date.)

The students themselves were conscious of being 'different'. One old student, Jessie Barrett, looked back sixty years to her schooldays at Queen's 1877–87 in a letter written during the Second World War:

> When I was a I Junior High Schools were beginning, and anyone who did not come up to our standard of behaviour, was told she had better go to a High School . . . I don't think anyone nowadays can quite realise what Queen's meant to us in those days, as we were so proud of the fact that we worked because we *wanted* to, and weren't just schoolgirls being made to.

Plumptre resigned finally in 1877 after forty years' service to Queen's. His place was now taken again by Llewelyn Davies, who was prepared to have another attempt at reforming and reorganising the College.

Llewelyn Davies was one of the most energetic and far-seeing of the Principals of Queen's. He wanted the College to provide a comprehensive education for girls from the age of eight to twenty-one, and hoped to see two stages in the College course, one leading to the matriculation examination of London University, and another to the degree examination.

There were many stumbling-blocks to the plan envisaged by Llewelyn Davies. One was social; many parents were not prepared to allow their daughters to continue receiving education after the age of seventeen or eighteen, because that was the age at which they should go into 'society', to enjoy themselves and to find a husband. A girl would need to be quite determined to defy convention and continue studying: the first undergraduates were exceedingly determined individuals. Llewelyn Davies told an audience of students and friends of Queen's in 1879 that

> it has been the disappointing experience of Queen's College from the first that the majority of its pupils have left the College, or have ceased to be more than occasional attendants at its lectures, before they have even passed through our Four Years' course.

although, he maintained

> a girl who discontinues regular study at seventeen or eighteen has not yet used her best opportunities.[1]

Another stumbling block as far as Queen's was concerned was that this plan was based on preparation for examinations. Was this in the spirit of Queen's? In the same lecture, Llewelyn Davies deplored an over-competitive atmosphere, and the presentation and acceptance of knowledge as a means of gaining marks. Yet both he and even more his sister insisted that if girls were serious in their desire for education, a standard must be set and aspired to. Llewelyn Davies again told his audience that to dispense with examinations

> would be no security for the preservation of the higher spirit of study. An examination is a guide to both teacher and pupil; it serves as a convenient goal; it is the only available test of diligence and sound knowledge: it applies a constant stimulus to flagging industry. With all its defects and dangers—and I think I am not insensible to them—a system of examination seems to me indispensable as instrumental machinery for the education of the many.

But that did not mean that everyone agreed with him.

Queen's had, after much argument, submitted its pupils to special examinations set by the Cambridge examiners since 1875. On the whole the reports had been good, though the weaknesses of the lecture system were exposed. The examiners in 1878 noted that

> the strong subjects were those where the lectures alone will impart a competent knowledge, the weak ones those where a large amount of home study is needed to supplement the class instruction.

A third stumbling block to the scheme was finance. Queen's

[1] The lecture was called *Fifty Years' Progress in Female Education* and was printed in the *Queen's College Calendar*, 1879–80.

had no substantial endowments and depended entirely on the fees for its income. The extensive repairs necessary to the property during 1874 had caused a deficit from which the College took many years to recover. An additional course which might not be well-supported was a financial risk.

In spite of these difficulties, the College had already arranged special courses of lectures during 1876 'to meet the needs of adult students'. These had already been suggested by Llewelyn Davies before his first resignation, and the scheme was put into practice by Plumptre, who had earlier introduced the evening classes at King's. By the following year, there were four series of lectures established; on elementary Botany, by Professor Bentley of King's, on the literature of the reign of Elizabeth I by Plumptre, on the legislation of the previous fifty years, by Henry Craik, and on the geology and scenery of the British Isles by Henry Seeley. The following year, Greek History, Anatomy and the Moral Philosophy of Hume and Mill were added.

In 1878 the degree examinations for London University were opened to women. Queen's made plans for courses leading to matriculation and a B.A. degree, 'such courses to be suitable also for women who might not wish to attend the examination, and to include some subjects not directly required for it'. Soon, forty-nine students had enrolled for these lectures.

So far as we know, only three students attending these lectures took the degree, in 1882; they were Margaret Topham, Edith Thompson and Hilda Miall. They supplemented the Queen's course, at the Principal's suggestion, by attending the lectures in Anglo-Saxon at University College. Edith Thompson was appointed a tutor at Queen's, and wore her gown as a symbol of her emancipation.

These higher lectures were not discontinued, but they were no longer described as a complete preparation for the degree examinations. In 1882, sixty-three students enrolled for them; in 1885 there were sixteen series of lectures, given by as many professors.

This was the point at which the College really had to decide whether it was going to be part of a university or not. University College opened its lectures to women generally in 1868, and after

1878 was definitely offering them degree courses; King's first admitted them in 1881, when the separate department for the Higher Education of Women was opened. The Queen's College Annual Report for 1882 referred to these changes:

> . . . the lectures at University College have been recently thrown open to women and largely attended by them. It would be impossible for Queen's College, except by an outlay quite beyond its means, to compete with the ample provision of teaching thus offered to students who seek the B.A. degree.
> This action on the part of University College illustrates the new phase on which female education has entered. Queen's College has now to encounter the rivalry of other schools and colleges having aims as high as its own.

Finance remained a great problem. But even if there had been enough money, one wonders if students intent on a university course would have chosen to take it in an institution which also educated small children. This seems to have been one great weakness of the plan. A complete separation of the School and College would have been necessary. Yet when the Council suggested a break at the age of sixteen, with a school for the younger pupils under a headmistress, the Committee of Education threw out the suggestion. The courses now offered at both Cambridge and Oxford, and the two London colleges, offered a more attractive prospect. They were set more clearly in the context of a university—a place where learning was advanced and individual study encouraged.

Not that other colleges found everything smooth. In Manchester, for example, an influential committee failed to persuade Owen's College (nucleus of the future university) to allow women to attend its lectures; instead they opened the Manchester and Salford College for Women, where Owen's College lecturers promised to teach. It opened in 1877 and forty-two girls enrolled. But progress was slow and disappointing. As so frequently had happened at Queen's, the students were dilatory and unambitious; only six girls obtained certificates awarded for three years' attendance at certain prescribed classes. When women were admitted to the lectures at Owen's College, the majority (called 'ladies') still attended only single courses of lectures, while a small minority (called 'women') registered for a full degree course.[1]

Bedford's experience was very similar to that of Queen's. The College started advanced lectures as soon as London University opened its degree examinations to women. There were three graduates in 1881. But as at Queen's, the degree students were a minority of those attending the advanced lectures, and the total number of students declined. It was just as discouraging for Bedford as for Queen's. One can only assume that there was more resolution and determination and faith amongst the governing body of Bedford than at Queen's. Two things really gave Bedford the impetus it needed in the 1890s; a Treasury grant to steady its shaky finances, and a full-time woman Principal to inspire and encourage its students. By 1900 half of the students at Bedford were preparing for graduation, and the College had become a school of the University.

What sort of course were the students offered at Queen's? The standard varied tremendously. The best lectures, as in the early days of Queen's, were quite up to the standard of those given in universities; the only difficulty was that the students were not always equal to understanding and appreciating them. In 1881, for example, there were several outstanding teachers. The history lecturer was John de Soyres, recently down from Cambridge. At Cambridge he won the Hulsean Prize with an essay on *Montanism and the Primitive Church*, which had already been published when he came to Queen's. He offered a series of lectures in the Higher Course on the History of the French Reformed Church 1659–1685; he was a scholarly and lively teacher.

John de Soyres was the inspiration of one of the most brilliant students Queen's has ever had, Gertrude Bell. There is a fascinating description of life at Queen's through her eyes, in *The Earlier*

[1] See Mabel Tylecote, *The Education of Women at Manchester University* (1941).

Letters of Gertrude Bell.[1] During some of the classes, Gertrude Bell was happy to write letters to members of her family; but not during a History lesson. She wrote to her stepmother:

> Tomorrow is my History lecture day. I should think he will give us a paper this time. I like him more than ever this term. He takes such broad views, never in the least one-sided, and he never says this is so but puts the two sides and tells one to choose. That's how history ought to be taught.

The height of her ambition was to be given 'excellent' by Mr de Soyres, and she put all her abundant energies into writing essays for him. In the same letter, she said:

> I've been very deep in my History questions. It is to trace the fluctuations in the actual power of the Monarchy from the Restoration to the Accession of George I. It's rather difficult to *write*. I think I understand it all—I ought to for I've read piles, literally piles of books about it—but it is so difficult to put it in a satisfactory form. I've written it twice but I think I shall re-write it before I give it up to Mr de Soyres.

He was very shy. When he first began his Higher course, Gertrude Bell and another girl were the only two to attend:

> It was a few minutes before the time, so we stood chatting before the fire when suddenly in came Mr Soyres. (He is most dreadfully [shy] I must tell you, but dreadfully.) Of course as there were only two girls he ought to have postponed the lecture, but he was much too frightened for that. He sat down and quickly began to lecture. We felt rather awkward, came away from the fire, sat down and began to take notes. The whole class consisted of Maude, Mr de Soyres and myself, and he was much more frightened of us than we of him.

[1] Edited by Elsa Richmond (1937).

She was able to tell her parents the following week that Mr de Soyres had had a large attendance at his next class.

In her last term (1886), Gertrude Bell attended a party given by Miss Croudace, the Lady Resident. Mr de Soyres was there too. Some of his shyness must have evaporated, for he asked his brilliant pupil if she was thinking of continuing her studies after taking the Queen's associateship. She told him of her ambition to go to Girton. He encouraged her immediately and said he had always longed for one of his pupils to take the history tripos. In fact, she went to Lady Margaret Hall at Oxford, impressed her contemporaries as 'the most brilliant student we ever had at Lady Margaret Hall',[1] and gained an excellent first in History.

On English Literature, the lecturer was Henry Morley, a former journalist and now also a professor at King's. He offered a series of lectures in the Higher course on English Literature from the birth of Wordsworth to 1815; this was no doubt the section of the comprehensive history of English Literature on which he was working at the time. He had been a collaborator of Dickens and had published numerous books. He was regarded more as a populariser than a great scholar, but was an excellent teacher.

As far as Science was concerned, it was possible to listen to lectures from eminent scholars. Henry Seeley was the Professor of Geology and Geography. He had already worked in the University Geological Museum at Cambridge assisting Adam Sedgwick. He was a Fellow of the Royal Society and had published several books on Geology and Palaeontology. Unfortunately as a teacher he was learned but dull.

Professor Thomson of King's taught Chemistry in the cavernous depths which served as a laboratory. His classes were very popular. One of those who attended was Mrs Lovibond (Frederica Fleay). She had been a student at Queen's twenty-three years previously but now (1882) returned to learn Chemistry so that she could help her husband to brew pure beer as economically as possible. As a result of attending these and other classes at University College, she gained the Bronze Medal for Brewing in the

[1] See Janet Courtney, *An Oxford Portrait Gallery* (1931).

City of London Guilds. The instruction proved even more useful to her after her husband's death, for she became the Managing Director and Chairman of Henry Lovibond and Sons Ltd.

The German classes were not inspiring. Gertrude Bell wrote many of her letters in them; for example:

> We are bored to death in this class, and we never learn anything . . . Dr Weil is so ugly, and he always wears a dirty shirt. I have never never seen him in a clean shirt yet. He smells of tobacco and he comes and pats you on the hand when you answer wrong (which invariably you do) and calls you his 'dear child'. He always addresses us as his 'dear children'.

There were complaints about him, but he always managed to get himself restored to favour. When summoned before the Council to explain why he had not appointed a Lady Assistant, he 'expressed his conviction that from the time of the appointment of lady teachers the College had begun to decline in efficiency and prosperity'.

Professor Cock had been teaching Mathematics at Queen's now for thirty-five years, and had passed his prime. There were complaints from the Lady Visitors and unfavourable comments from the Cambridge examiners. The same complaints were made about Francis Garden, the Professor of Theology, also elderly. Both agreed to resign in 1883. Professor Cock had been one of the best-loved teachers of the College, and was very successful in his prime. Camilla Croudace wrote his epitaph in the magazine:

> Kindliness, courtesy, sympathy and genuine humour were his characteristics to the very end, added to a most sincere love of, and devotion to, Queen's College.

The year before, John Hullah resigned, after thirty years of teaching music at the College. The last links with the foundation of the College were being severed. John Hullah died in 1884 and Thomas Astley Cock in 1885.

A crisis over the government of the College led to the resignation of Llewelyn Davies. There were repeated suggestions that the Council and Committee of Education should unite, and an appeal was made to the Visitor to arbitrate between their varying claims and rights. A stalemate ensued. Finally, the Principal announced his resignation, and approved the intention of other members of the Council to do the same. At the end of 1885, the Council unanimously resolved:

> That the Visitor be informed that it is almost certain that the Council will cease to exist in the course of next Term, and be requested to take the preliminary legal step which will be necessary. Also that the Council regard favourably a suggestion that this College be annexed to King's College.

The last is an interesting suggestion of which nothing more was heard. Certain members of the Council, including the Dowager Lady Stanley of Alderley, a veteran of the 'women's movement', and Mrs Garrett Anderson, did resign; others remained, including Anna Swanwick, and nominated new members.

Llewelyn Davies resigned and shortly left London to become the Vicar of Kirby Lonsdale. His successor at Queen's was Canon Elwyn.

X

1886–1900. The End of the Century

QUEEN'S was not destined to become a college of any university, although the idea of amalgamating with an existing college of London University was several times suggested before 1914. The practice of giving 'higher' lectures, and lectures for the general public, refused to die. By 1900 the College had established a tradition of a broad and liberal education, preparing some for further study at university, and giving others a final preparation for entry into professional, social and domestic life. In 1898 the College celebrated its Jubilee and could look back on fifty years' achievement; fifty years in which the whole position of women in society had changed.

By 1900, women were largely assuming responsibility for the education of girls. In the girls' high schools already established all over the country, women alone formed the staff. Queen's was more conservative, and had not yet appointed a woman professor, nor yet contemplated a woman principal. Many former students, in looking back, appreciated the lectures they received from the men professors. But they also appreciated the influence of the highly individual women who were given authority in the College.

Foremost among these was Camilla Croudace, the Lady Resident from 1881 until 1906. She was an old student of the College, an admirer of its founder, and a person who largely devoted her life to its service. She was respected and admired by all those under her care. Her lace cap, her regal bearing and her sense of humour were familiar to generations of students.

Camilla Croudace had travelled a great deal. Even before she entered Queen's as a school pupil in 1856 she had spent much time with her grandfather in Kiev, where he was building a bridge over the Dnieper. After leaving Queen's, she was a governess for a short while, and then travelled with her family on the continent. After a year spent teaching at Kensington High School, she came to Queen's as Lady Resident in 1881.

Her family was Swedenborgian, and though she was not herself a practising member of that sect, she impressed the students as a 'very spiritual person'. She took prayers in the Waiting Room every morning. At lunch time she presided in the dining-room, and all students had to bow to her on leaving and say 'prosit' (without, for the most part, knowing why). Her quiet but firm emphasis on 'the right spirit' always secured good behaviour without scolding. She was not an intellectual woman and did no teaching, but was rather a person of wisdom and good judgment whose influence pervaded the whole life of the College.

She did not confine her influence or efforts to the hours of instruction. In the evenings she would sometimes entertain her friends in the College and invite some of the girls to act as hostesses. At the week-ends she would often invite girls to visit Ridgecap, her country cottage in Surrey, and even sometimes allow them to go there on their own, with Ella, her maid, doing the cooking. Mrs Murphy (Evelyn Payne 1896–1903) remembers her favourite phrase of 'Bundle, bundle, bundle off to bed!' during those wonderful week-ends, when talk could go on for ever. During the holidays, she organised walking parties which were always popular.

Mademoiselle Séguin was a French teacher who spent a few hours each week at Queen's. She was an extraordinary and unforgettable character, with a vivid imagination and a histrionic flair. Her youth was spent in Paris and she remembered, she said, eating rats and men's beards during the Paris Commune. When she came to England, she delighted in being invited to country house parties. Having been warned by her mother that 'man was a dangerous animal', her triumph was unbounded when she found that the ladies preferred listening to her recite to going fishing or riding with the men. When the ladies appeared at dinner with 'boiled eyes', so overcome with emotion at her performance, the men, she said, were *furious*. At Queen's, where she taught French from 1878 until 1911, her popularity was such that she declared it to have been almost one person's work to carry all the flowers which were given to her—until Miss Croudace stopped the practice.

Her pupils regarded her as an excellent teacher, though they found her methods a little unconventional. Every one was addressed by the name 'Dolly', and anyone who used a handkerchief in her presence was given the instant order 'Pocket Dolly', for Mademoiselle Séguin was terrified of germs. All windows had to be kept closed for the same reason. She was enveloped in clothes, with just the tip of her nose apparently peeping out of a multitude of scarves, so that she was most aptly described as 'a walking wardrobe'. She returned her pupils' exercise books by throwing them, and woe betide anyone who failed to catch her own.

The Council minutes are full of her complaints about salary and conditions of service. She exasperated the Council perpetually, but on all occasions except one, agreed at the last moment to accept their terms. In 1911, however, she positively refused to move her teaching-room so that a students' common room could be made. This time the Council and the Committee of Education yielded not an inch to her threats and requests, and her proffered resignation was accepted. 'Therefore,' she wrote, 'though reluctantly and with a broken heart, I must give up a situation, which for thirty-three years has been the privilege, the glory, the aim, the love, and bread of my life.'

When she retired, Mrs Murphy (Evelyn Payne) went with her to spend her presentation money on furniture for her new small flat:

> Never could I forget the experience! Hours and hours were spent just sitting and looking at the objects she set her heart on, while she bargained for price-reductions—perspiring profusely—it was a very hot summer—and resorting to dramatic tears to get her way. Eventually she got all she wanted and was delighted and grateful. We understood she was very hard up. But when she died her will was published in the London papers, as she had left all her savings—a surprisingly big sum, to the French Church in Leicester Square!

Miss Kilgour and Miss Luard were also excellent teachers. Miss Kilgour taught mathematics, for twenty-five years, from 1880 until 1905. She lived to be over a hundred and died only in 1955. Miss Luard had studied at Lady Margaret Hall, Oxford, and became headmistress of the School in 1895. She encouraged her pupils to find things out for themselves, and to cultivate a good literary style. Some of them would search for hours in Roget's *Thesaurus* to find the exact word required.

Amongst the professors, two names stand out beyond all the others—John Adam Cramb and Walter Rippmann. As one former student put it, Professor Cramb was the best lecturer and Professor Rippmann was the best teacher. Every old student who has written or spoken about these years was impressed by these teachers.

John Adam Cramb was the Professor of History at Queen's from 1893 until his death in 1913. During these years he lectured at Queen's on two days a week, combining this with writing and lecturing elsewhere. He made a lasting impression on those who heard him.

He was a native of Scotland and studied Classics at Glasgow University. He gained first-class honours and won other academic distinctions. After a period of study in Germany he returned to Glasgow as a lecturer in Modern History. But soon he felt the pull of London. His ambition was to establish himself as an author and the stimulation and contacts which London could provide seemed essential to him. He settled in Kensington, began to write for serious journals and for the Dictionary of National Biography, and looked round for opportunities to lecture. After two years, in 1892, Harold Cox, editor of the *Edinburgh Review*, appointed Cramb as his deputy at Queen's; a year later Cox resigned and Cramb was appointed his successor as Professor of History.

For the next twenty years, Queen's provided him with a secure revenue, with a platform for his ideas and with a means of making contact with the social and intellectual world of London. Through invitations to the homes of some of his students, he began to give short courses of lectures in private houses, and continued to do this for the rest of his life.

He is recorded as saying:

> No action or effort is so painful or so hard as thought. Hence the vast majority of men and women never think. It is too painful.

He made it his business to stimulate his pupils to think. One of his students, Lilian Rigby, took down his lectures in shorthand and later transcribed them into longhand. Her notebooks, twenty of them, were later given to the College. They were also used as the basis for the published version of some of Cramb's lectures, because he used no notes in his lectures. Later on, Lilian Rigby married Charles Russell. And a few years before she died, she wrote a life of her beloved teacher.[1] There she says of his teaching:

> Cramb began his career as a lecturer to girls with the Renaissance, and at once captivated their attention by the passionate earnestness of his manner and the unaccustomed methods of his teaching. History, for these fortunate students, was to be no longer a dull progression of Western European wars, legislation, politics and diplomacy, accessions and deaths of sovereigns and the like, with class instruction supplemented by the study of one or two text-books entitled *A Short History of—*. For their new professor took all history and all epochs for his sphere, including painting, music, philosophy, religion, in fact the whole of life, in his range. The problems of European history, for example, led him to Persia, to Arabia, to North Africa, whilst English history of necessity involved an intensive study of India.

She gives examples of the subjects he used to set for essays and the books he expected his students to use in preparation. For example, for an essay on 'Charlemagne and the Year 800', he

[1] Mrs Charles E. B. Russell, *John Adam Cramb. Patriot, Historian, Mystic* (1950).

prescribed Gibbon's *Decline and Fall of the Roman Empire*, Milman's *Latin Christianity*, Bryce's *Holy Roman Empire*, Montesquieu's *De l'Esprit des Lois, La Chanson de Roland* and Giesebrecht's *Geschichte der Deutschen Kaiserzeit.* For an essay on 'Lorenzo dei Medici', he prescribed Roscoe's *Life of Lorenzo* and Machiavelli's *History of Florence.* He did not make much reference to the essay subjects in his lectures, so that the students' own written work had to be based on wide reading. And we have it on the testimony of several of his own old students that they at least did this reading, under the influence of his own enthusiasm and original thinking. He would always give a choice of subjects, and encouraged the students to develop their own interests.

In order to encourage extensive and unusual reading, Cramb used to go to the London Library and borrow at least ten volumes at a time for the use of his Queen's students. He did this for example when he spent a whole term on Indian history. The outside examiner for History was York Powell, who said that the Queen's History papers were more interesting than any others he had to mark.

Cramb also took the opportunity to deliver afternoon lectures at Queen's which were open to the public. In 1899, he gave a series of seven lectures, inspired by his own reactions to both the Dreyfus case in France, and the South African war in which Britain was then involved. The lectures were then published as *The Origins and Destiny of Imperial Britain.* This book did not receive many good reviews, though it later ran into a second edition. It was controversial, almost polemical, passionate, painted on a broad canvas. It was prophetic too; he urged then, as he did over the following years, that Germany was the arch enemy of England.

This theme was followed again in a series of lectures given at Queen's in 1913, and published in the year following, posthumously, as *Germany and England.* This book ran into thirteen editions within a year. Its author attempted to explain something of 'the German mind' and prophesied that 'the friendly rivalry' which some people talked of between Germany and England had more tragic possibilities. His views were founded on his own deep reading and on his own experiences as a young student in Germany—a country he had visited before even coming to England.

Cramb's career was really based on his connection with Queen's. Many people believed he should have achieved a greater eminence than ever came his way, and that he should have been offered some further academic position or honour. They did not all know that he was offered a post as Professor of History at King's in 1902, but turned it down because he would not subscribe to the Thirty-Nine Articles; years earlier a similar intellectual scrupulousness had led him to abandon his studies for the Presbyterian ministry. Perhaps he was too subjective in his approach, too much committed to causes to place all his hopes on an academic career. For the last six years of his life he worked closely with Lord Roberts, writing speeches for him and campaigning with him for the introduction of national service. One other position he did take on towards the end of his life, that of lecturer at the Staff College in Camberley. But then his career was cut short by his early death in 1913 at the age of fifty-two.

Walter Rippmann (he changed it to Ripman during the First World War) was a few years younger than John Cramb. He applied for the post of Professor of German in 1896, when he was twenty-seven, and was able to present an impressive battery of qualifications, having taken the Tripos Examinations at Cambridge in Classics, Medieval and Modern Languages and Indian Languages, with first- or second-class honours in each. He was chosen from forty applicants, accepted the position, and stayed for nearly twenty years.

Walter Rippmann was an admirer of Oscar Wilde, of Walter Pater, and of *art nouveau*. In contrast to most of the other professors, he was 'young and ardent', and a man of great social charm. With his more able original students, he was ready to spend time in stimulating conversation, introducing them to new ideas and encouraging them to discover their own potentialities. A select group was invited to visit his home in Ladbroke Grove, where he would talk to them of his literary heroes, show them his collection of Japanese prints, and introduce them to an exciting new world.

He was a great experimenter in methods of teaching German

(and later of other languages too) and used a special phonetic alphabet to help his students to acquire a good accent. He insisted wherever possible that they spoke only in German; they had to describe some large pictures of 'Seasons in Germany', put up on the wall of the German room, opposite the Chemistry laboratory. Throughout his life he wrote an enormous number of books, most of them modern language primers published by Dents. These he tried out on his students, much to their advantage.

Another lecturer who later achieved great distinction, but who found little favour with his Queen's students at the time was Richard Gregory, who was appointed the Professor of Astronomy in 1897, and remained until 1918. Many of the students apparently affected to despise him because they said he had a 'common accent'. This was their loss, because the students who did attend his lectures found them fascinating. The lectures he organised for the general public were very much better attended. He later became Astronomer Royal. Throughout his career he was a friend of H. G. Wells, who consulted him constantly for both personal and scientific advice.

Then there was Professor Seeley, whose lectures tended to be dull but who led fascinating geological expeditions, and Professor Hall Griffin who was held in esteem because he had been a friend of Browning and specialised in lecturing on *The Ring and the Book*.

The Principals, Canon Elwyn (1886–95) and the Rev C. J. Robinson (1895–9) were more shadowy figures who made much less impression on the students. Canon Elwyn in particular was much liked in the College; but was known better by the staff than by the students. He taught Theology once a week and attended committee meetings most conscientiously, combining these duties with a multitude of other interests and responsibilities. He was Master of the Charterhouse, and occasionally entertained some of the senior students there.

There was opportunity at Queen's for a real education, for intellectual stimulation and for a great widening of horizons. But it was left very much to the individual student to decide whether or not to work. The College did not turn out any kind of model pupil. On the contrary, there was an infinite variety in the

5a J. A. Cramb, Professor of Modern History 1893–1913

5b Walter Rippmann
Professor of German 1896–1912

5c Joseph Edwards
Principal 1919–31

6a Miss G. E. Holloway, Principal 1932–40

6b Miss A. M. Kynaston, Principal 1942–64

characters and later achievements of the students. The most important thing was that there was always room for the individualist who found it hard to fit into a more conventional or stereotyped atmosphere; Gertrude Bell and Sophia Jex-Blake, for instance, When such a person found a teacher to match her own ability, as Gertrude Bell did in Professor de Soyres, then the College achieved a great success.

The other great point in favour of Queen's was that it was not a copy of a boys' public school. The very earliest staff of the College, Maurice and Kingsley, for example, had themselves had no first-hand experience of public schools, and this was true of many of the later Professors. Unlike some of the high schools which took boys' schools for their model, Queen's remained strikingly aloof from this development. There was no cult of sport either, though callisthenics had found a place in the curriculum.

In 1898 the College celebrated its Jubilee. A distinguished old student. Mrs Alec Tweedie (Ethel Harley 1877–9) produced a Jubilee Book, *The First College for Women: memories and records of work done 1848–98*, consisting largely of reminiscences of earlier years and articles on work being done by former students. The authors could look back to 1848, when 'to have lost money was considered all that was necessary to prepare a woman for earning a salary', and consider what great strides had been made since then. For example, Octavia Lewin wrote of her experiences as a house surgeon, Louisa Twining of her work as a Poor Law Guardian, and Mrs Lovibond (Frederica Fleay) on *How I became a managing director*. The book remains excellent source material for anyone interested in the social history of the second half of the nineteenth century.

The Queen[1] observed in its review of the book:

> No other women's college would have produced a book like this. The students of younger colleges, which set before themselves University standards of intellectual competence, would probably have written a book more free than this

[1] May 28 1898.

> from unscholarly and slipshod English and worn out classical tags, but we do not believe they could show an equal degree of variety of characters and occupations. They would write, almost without exception, in a certain tone—the academic and educational—but Queen's College girls appear to have no one tone. Queen's College would seem to awaken the minds of its students to countless possibilities, and to leave its young women to choose their own work.

One former student who did not write in the Jubilee book was the actress Florence Farr, though another actress who was her contemporary, Mrs Beerbohm Tree (they were both at Queen's in the 1870s) wrote a vivid account of her memories of Queen's. Florence Farr had just broken off her friendship with Shaw, and was beginning her friendship with Yeats, who wrote many plays for her. Her book, *Modern Woman: her intentions*, published in 1910, revealed her as one of the decidedly more unconventional students of Queen's.

The actual Jubilee celebrations took place during the first week of May 1898. There were lectures, a service and a ball and there was endless reminiscing. The Queen was invited to call at the College during the festivities. No word was heard and the week went past. But in the early afternoon of May 9 a message arrived to say that the Queen would stop outside the College during the course of her afternoon drive. The students were hurriedly sent home to put on their white dresses, and a few of the Lady Visitors who lived in the neighbourhood were summoned. These and the staff who happened to be present that afternoon gathered outside or at the windows. The Queen 'beamed with health and smiles, and was surmounted by a bonnet all plumed and trimmed with white, while even her sunshade was more grey than black in hue . . .'[1] The Principal gave the Queen a loyal address while the Queen's Scholar, Kathleen Croudace, presented her with a basket of roses. The scene is perpetuated for the benefit of those studying in the Waiting Room by a painting by Ella Bedford, the drawing

[1] *Modern Society* May 21, 1898.

teacher. What the Queen herself thought of the institution and its achievements we do not know—except that the subject of 'Women's Rights' did not meet with her approval.

The old students who returned for the Jubilee celebrations found the building changed. The old front door of no 45 had been altered to a window, leaving no 43 as the one main entrance. Passing through the new inner screen doors, one now faced a long wide corridor leading to a new large hall (the Pfeiffer Hall) with new classrooms for the School underneath. The staircase of 43 was removed and wrought iron railings were fixed round the well hole bereft of stairs. It struck a young niece of Miss Croudace what a suitable place it would make for keeping a giraffe; hence its name, 'the giraffe hole'. Unfortunately the L.C.C. fire regulations later required that it should be glassed over. The archway and flight of steps now leading to the main staircase of 45 were christened 'the Rialto'. These improvements were made possible through the bequest of Mrs Ida Pfeiffer, and executed by the architect Percy Newton. Though some of the familiar landmarks had disappeared, the Waiting Room, with its beautiful moulded ceiling, and the Library, with its atmosphere conducive to study, remained as central features of College life.

XI

1900–14. Tradition Maintained

THE years 1900 to 1914 have been described as years of 'immense ferment' and 'restless fertility'.[1] If there was ferment at Queen's, it was well hidden; nowhere was the existing social order so well preserved. But intellectual excitement and challenge were there for those who could take advantage of them.

The first few years of the century are especially connected with the name of Katherine Mansfield, probably the most gifted creative artist who has so far passed through Queen's. Whether or not one can go as far as Antony Alpers and call her a 'writer of genius',[2] she is certainly amongst the greatest of short story writers in the English language. Her art and her life were intertwined, and the forging and refining of both began at Queen's.

Katherine Mansfield (her real name was Kathleen Beauchamp) and her two sisters entered Queen's in April 1903. Their parents lived in New Zealand, but sent the three girls to England, accompanied by their young aunt, Belle Dyer, to continue and finish their education. The Beauchamps' cousins, Sylvia and Evelyn Payne, were already at Queen's, and Harold Beauchamp decided to send his own daughter to the College thus recommended.

The Beauchamps were boarders, that is, they boarded with Clara Wood, who leased no 41 and the upper part of 43 Harley Street, with just over twenty students living in. All girls shared rooms, and the Beauchamps were lucky to share a room between them. From part of their quarters, the boarders could look down through the giraffe hole into the corridor below, and watch life being enacted there.

Miss Clara Finetta Wood had kept a boarding house since 1873

[1] R. C. K. Ensor, *England 1870–1914* (1936) p. 557.

[2] See Antony Alpers, *Katherine Mansfield* (1954).

and was quite an institution; she was now elderly and always wore purple—except when she went to the opera and then it was lavender. She must have had a great preoccupation with purple or violet, because the address from which she applied for the post in 1873 was 'Violet Cottage, Felixstowe', and in later years she used violet ink. Her hair was another noticeable feature about her. She wore a large coil to make up for her own thin endowment of hair; to cover the place where the two joined, she wore a velvet band—adorned with a simple bow during the day, but in the evening by sequins and beads, which were fascinating to many of her charges.

Her students would go into the College dining-room for breakfast, then go for a crocodile walk to Park Square Gardens, for which Queen's was privileged to have a special key, or to Regent's Park to feed the squirrels and ducks. After this they joined the other students in the College. At the end of the afternoon session they went for another walk, usually to the Gardens, where in summer they played tennis and croquet. They returned to the Boarding House to change, went downstairs for an hour's silent study from 6.0 until 7.0, and then to the Waiting Room for dinner. After this, Clara Wood used to come downstairs to collect her girls and liked to read to them from some edifying Victorian novel. She liked to invite them to come into her private sitting-room, on the second floor immediately above the present Principal's office. It was a cluttered but welcoming room. 'The general effect was a warm cosiness of crimson and wine colour and flickering firelight and one instantly felt at home' (Dr Patricia Shaw). At the week-ends, she encouraged her charges to visit museums, churches and the older parts of London. The boarders appreciated the fact that they were not looked after in the evenings by staff who had taught them during the day, and they were able to relax more freely in the precious half-hour at the end of the day.

Katherine Mansfield formed the most permanent relationship she ever knew while she was at Queen's. It was with the girl who showed her to her room on the very first day, though the friendship did not begin for several weeks. Ida Baker was already a friend of Evelyn and Sylvia Payne. She was a retiring, shy and unsophisticated girl, who was surprised when one of the Beauchamps met her on the staircase one day and said 'Let's be friends'; she was taken aback, but responsive. That friendship lasted until Katherine Mansfield's death. It was an unusual one, regarded with a certain amount of disapproval by many contemporaries, Katherine Mansfield was already a rebellious, highly individual non-conformist. She would look out of the window of her bedroom, announcing to her assembled friends, 'Don't bother me girls, I'm going to have a mood'. Those who were not her particular friends, on the whole, disliked her. Ida Baker was a complement to Katherine Mansfield. Where Katherine Mansfield liked to dominate, Ida Baker enjoyed acting as a friend, helpmate and even devotee of a gifted and individual rebel.

Ida Baker has, forty-five years after the death of her friend, written of her vivid memories of her youth.[1] She gives a clue to Katherine Mansfield's apparent detachment and play-acting:

> She once said that even in moments of most intense living there was always a part of herself which stood aside, looking on, noting all. Though I found this hard to understand, it was true for her.

And her astonishing maturity is revealed here:

> To find Truth, Katherine said, she would go down into herself, deep down, like sinking to the bottom of a dark well. Waiting at the bottom, Truth would come to her. Katherine knew this when she was only fourteen years old . . .

Katherine was very musical and played the 'cello. For a time she believed that music was her vocation. But even earlier she had decided to become a writer, and her musical ambitions were in the end short-lived. Both Katherine and Ida Baker decided to adopt *noms de plume* for future use. Katherine chose 'Katherine Mansfield', Mansfield being her grandmother's maiden name and

[1] *Katherine Mansfield: The memories of L.M.*, Michael Joseph (1971).

her own second name. Ida Baker took 'Lesley Moore', and figures in Katherine Mansfield's *Journal* as LM.

Katherine Mansfield wrote five stories for the College Magazine within a space of two years. She astonished the editor with the maturity of her style. The latest one, *About Pat,* which came out in December 1905 was the best: 'an experience of childhood directly and vividly described, with an eye for significant detail and a touch in characterisation which for the first time can be said to have belonged to Katherine Mansfield.'[1]

Queen's provided Katherine Mansfield with a much richer store of friendships than she had found in New Zealand. Holidays with her old-fashioned great aunt and uncle were a trial, and sometimes her aunt, Belle Dyer, who had taken the position of assistant to Clara Wood, caused storms by trying to exercise too strict a supervision. But for most of the time Katherine Mansfield pursued her friendships with the utmost seriousness, and through them, began to develop her acute observation of the human condition.

One of the professors really inspired her—Walter Rippmann, the Professor of German. She was one of the select circle of students with whom he would talk after his lecture, and whom he invited to visit his home. Here she was introduced to the ideas of Oscar Wilde, and to a whole new world of art and literature. She adored Walter Rippmann. After she had been at Queen's for two terms, she wrote to her cousin Sylvia Payne:

> I am *ashamed* at the way in which I long for German. I simply can't help it. It is dreadful. And when I go into class I feel I must just stare at him the whole time.

She did not do particularly well in examinations; but then examinations are not suited to testing the individually brilliant. One of her reports described her work in English Language as 'unsatisfactory' and in English Literature as 'disappointing'. She herself admitted, however, that she wasted many of her opportunities. She later wrote in her *Journal*:

[1] Antony Alpers, *Katherine Mansfield* (1954), p. 69.

> I was thinking yesterday of my *wasted, wasted* early girlhood. My college life, which is such a vivid and detailed memory in one way, might never have contained a book or a lecture. I lived in the girls, the professors, the big, lovely building, the leaping fires in winter and the abundant flowers in summer. The views out of the windows, all the pattern that was—weaving. Nobody saw it, I felt, as I did. My mind was just like a squirrel. I gathered and gathered and hid away, for that long 'winter' when I should rediscover all this treasure—and if anybody came close I scuttled up the tallest, darkest tree and hid in the branches. And I was so awfully fascinated in watching Hall Griffin and all his tricks—thinking about him as he sat there, his private life, what he was like as a man etc., etc. (He told us he and his brother once wrote an enormous poem called the Epic of the Hall Griffins.) Then it was only at rare intervals that something flashed through all this busyness, something about Spenser's Faerie Queene or Keats' Isabella or the Pot of Basil, and those flashes were always when I disagreed flatly with H.G. and wrote in my notes—This man is a fool. And Cramb, wonderful Cramb! The figure of Cramb was enough, he was 'history' to me. Ageless and fiery, eating himself up again and again, very fierce at what he had seen, but going a bit blind because he had looked so long. . . .
>
> But what coherent account could I give of the history of English Literature? And what of English History? None.[1]

Though she may have neglected some of her opportunities, she took an active part in College life. She joined the Debating Society and often spoke to the motions. She wrote for the College Magazine. Once she visited Ridgecap and wrote in the Visitors' Book: 'I have never spent happier holidays. Is there anything more beautiful than English woods in spring?'

The themes of Katherine Mansfield's stories were frequently

[1] Katherine Mansfield, *Journal*. Edited by J. Middleton Murry (1954). pp. 103–4.

concerned with her childhood and with New Zealand. But she did use her Queen's experiences occasionally. Walter Rippmann figured as 'The Wanderer' in *A Fairy Story*; and another story, *Carnation* is about a French lecture at Queen's.

Altogether her stay at Queen's proved a liberating experience for Katherine Mansfield, if a disturbing and frustrating one for some of her contemporaries.

We have seen that Queen's offered more than formal instruction. The societies were flourishing at this time. The Debating Society was founded in 1903, and has continued, with breaks, ever since. The first debate was on the motion, 'That music is the highest of the arts' and was carried by ten votes. The Swanwick Society, named after its founder Anna Swanwick, met every month. It was started as a result of Miss Swanwick's lecture on Poetry at the time of the College Jubilee in 1898. Each member was given a white notebook decorated in gold with the College badge, and into it copied any poem which specially impressed her. These poems were read out at the monthly meetings, and the members were encouraged to learn them by heart. The meetings were held in the evening, once a month; the students wore evening dress, and took refreshments together after the readings. Miss Croudace, one regrets to have to say, sometimes went to sleep during the proceedings.

The Dante Society was not confined to members of the College and had an outside committee; it met monthly to hear lectures by Dante experts. There was also an orchestra which gave concerts in the Portman Rooms. And the College Magazine flourished at this time.

The College was still rather conservative and old-fashioned in atmosphere, but few people wanted it to copy the model of the new girls' high schools. When Camilla Croudace retired as the Lady Resident in 1906 she wrote a pleading letter to the Principal:

> I do earnestly hope that the College will not depart from its ancient traditions and spirit, but will remain the unique institution which it has hitherto been. May all those of its pupils who pass through the four years course be able to

> say with me 'I am grateful to Queen's College for a liberal education which has taught me a sense of proportion and given me the patience necessary for dealing with men'. Dear Mr Principal you cannot perhaps quite realise what the College is to those who have been brought up within its walls but I am sure you will understand and sympathise with my desire to see it remaining itself and not becoming an unsuccessful imitation of modern schools.

Some changes had to come. Miss Croudace's successor, who was now called the Warden, applied for membership of the Headmistresses' Association, and an account of the College was put into the Girls' School Year Book. Miss Harper followed Miss Croudace for two years, and was then succeeded by Miss C. E. Lewer, a formidable and dignified woman who devoted herself to both the domestic and the educational affairs of the College for eighteen years (1908–26).

In the same week as Miss Lewer's appointment, the Lady Visitors were reminded that they were an *advisory* body; and the Council made sure that amongst the new Lady Visitors were several who had not been educated at Queen's, since they could view the College tradition with a more objective and critical eye.

Although the Committee of Education agreed in 1906 that 'no person shall be disqualified from being the Principal, a Professor or a special Member of the Committee . . . by reason of that person being a woman', there was no change in the masculine regime until 1931. The Principal from 1899 until 1904 was the Rev T. W. Sharpe, a former H.M.I. and Chief Inspector of the Education Department; from 1904 until 1912 it was Canon G. C. Bell, former Master of Marlborough College; and from 1912 until 1915 it was Sir Henry Craik, M.P., the first layman to be Principal. Each of these men was distinguished in his own field, but remained a shadowy figure to the students of the College.

The School was enjoying one of its best periods. Miss Luard and Miss Teale were the two headmistresses. Both of them had studied at Oxford; both were scholars and, in the best sense, devoted teachers. Miss Harper was the second mistress and gave exciting and unusual English lessons. One of her pupils (Dr Patricia Shaw) remembers her love of words; 'Once I missed a lesson on the word "mountebank" and to this day I feel deprived of the full knowledge about it.' Lessons took place in the morning only; those who chose to stayed in the afternoon, and they and the boarders did preparation.

There were at least five classes, and at one time seven, in the School. Pupils, girls and boys, were taken from the age of six; the boys were supposed to leave before they were nine. Miss Luard later described the School as consisting mainly 'of the children of the doctors around, of some actors and playwrights and of a few leading Jewish families. These children were, for the most part, eager, responsive and intelligent.'

The standard of the lectures in the College continued to be high, though whether they were really the best form of education for the girls of fourteen who had just left the School (or some other school) was debatable. The change from the School, with some excellent teachers, to the system of attending lectures given by men professors, who varied greatly in their capacity for interesting their audience, was considerable. The schoolgirl of fourteen now suddenly transformed into 'Miss X' the College student might find herself somewhat at sea; the College and School were so effectively segregated that she might think herself in a different establishment. At least one of the professors also doubted the value of the method. Professor Gregory wrote to the Principal in 1906 in tart vein, arguing that the standard of the entrance examination should be raised:

> Personally, my opinion is that most of the students now in the College ought to be in the School—which might be developed into a good type of High School—while the College ought to be filled with adults capable of understanding and appreciating the unique character of many of the lectures given by the professors. We are, under the present conditions, using steam hammers to crack nuts when they might be employed for much more powerful work.

His advice was not followed, and the professors continued to lecture to students of varied attainment. The best of them were so good that one believes that all students must have received something of value, though it was not always, as in the case of Katherine Mansfield, a systematic education.

The trouble was that there was only the remotest chance of most of the students having to earn their own livings. The majority of students were looking forward not to a university career, but to a year at a finishing school in France or Italy, the London season and presentation at Court. The students of this era who entered professions and attained academic or professional distinction are few; most of them entered the social life of their class and remained 'amateurs'. Those students who aspired to a university career needed special coaching in order to pass matriculation and were looked upon with some astonishment by their contemporaries. One student who aimed at a professional career and doubted the value of her education as a preparation for it was told by her tutor that her years at Queen's might prove a disadvantage in the short run, but an advantage in the long run; this she agrees her life has proved. Another student who valued her education at Queen's put it that 'the idea of Queen's was to teach us how to teach ourselves, rather than the amassing of facts'. Professor Cramb's lectures, and even more the essays he set, were an example of this. One could not avoid thinking if one was to satisfy Professor Cramb; a list of facts was unacceptable, and was rarely given; he stimulated his students to think. The 'History essay' played an important part in College life for everyone.

One has to admit that there was something undesirably snobbish in the atmosphere. This did not come from the professors and it had nothing to do with the influence of Maurice. It came from some of the students, whose parents in particular regarded the education of their daughters as something of a social investment; and from a few of the women teachers, who compensated for their own lack of qualifications with a belief in social exclusiveness.

In 1913 Professor Jack, the Professor of English, suggested that the I Juniors, the first year in the College, should be taught by the women teachers and that the professors should be allowed to give a fifth year of instruction in the College. A few months later, plans were made for a complete scheme of advanced lectures, and the professors were to be allowed to devote themselves entirely to this advanced work provided that there were enough students. But the war put an end to the scheme.

One subject was compulsory for everyone in the College: callisthenics. The Calendar firmly declared:

> In view of the importance of daily physical exercise it is arranged that half an hour shall be devoted by every Pupil to Callisthenics every day from 12.0 to 12.30. Miss Marshall-Burch is the Teacher. There can be no exemption (except in the case of temporary indisposition) without a doctor's certificate.

In fact it was really Mrs Marshall-Burch who conducted the lesson, and her daughter who helped. Mrs Marshall-Burch sat gracefully in an armchair, with a soft wrap round her. Miss Marshall-Burch stood like a ramrod and issued orders; she was not graceful, and looked like a Dutch doll. Most of the time, the students practised deportment and curtsying, though sometimes they learnt exhibition dances. It was not the favourite lesson.

When Mrs Marshall-Burch retired callisthenics continued but the curtsying came to an end. Miss Lamborn took a special dancing class as an 'extra', and in this class the students learnt gavottes and mazurkas, and practised 'positions'; they changed into white muslin or silk dresses with blue sashes and dancing pumps. As Miss Lamborn was 'one of Mrs Wordsworth's teachers', this class was socially very acceptable.

Two new courses were introduced in these years. The first was a Domestic Science course, introduced at the instigation of Mrs Waley-Cohen in 1901. It caused a furore at first and did not become a permanent course until much later. In 1910 the idea of a special course for foreign students was put forward, and began with a series of lectures given by Walter Rippmann on the pronunciation of English. Gradually a clientele of foreign students was built up, and by 1914 ten of them were taking a special course which included language, literature and history. Students of many nationalities came; a special relationship was built up with Norway and many Norwegian girls came over to take the course. In 1912, they came from France, Russia, Germany, Finland and Spain as well as Norway.

By the beginning of 1914 many of the familiar figures had disappeared. Professor Rippmann had resigned after almost twenty successful years of teaching, in 1912. Professor Cramb died suddenly the following year and his loss was keenly felt. The Principal of 1904–12, the Rev G. C. Bell, had retired and his place was taken by Sir Henry Craik. Clara Wood died in 1911, and her name is perpetuated by an annual[1] lecture established in her memory.

The years 1900–14 were lively years for Queen's, with much stimulating teaching and lecturing, with many eminent men contributing to the life of the College, and with students who felt themselves treated as individuals. 'Women's rights are upheld in the College, especially the right of talking', claimed the Magazine (1903).

[1] Now biennial.

XII

1914–32
The End of Masculine Dominance

THE First World War had little apparent effect on the life and structure of Queen's. Lectures, classes and the Boarding House continued much the same, and very few students were withdrawn because of the war; in 1917 the Headmistress of the School remarked on how few of the pupils had absented themselves on account of the air raids. Even the social changes brought about by the upheaval of the war were slow to manifest themselves at Queen's; the introduction of lectures on English Citizenship, 'in the hope that those to whom the franchise has recently been extended may qualify themselves to use their new opportunities aright' was the only sign of immediate change.

The new Principal in 1915, Professor Kendall, took a closer interest in the achievements of the College than some of his predecessors. He was a small, sharp-witted man, forthright but charming. He was already the Professor of History; he was also a clergyman, the Committee of Education having agreed that it was desirable to appoint a clergyman 'in accordance with the early traditions of the College' (Sir Henry Craik's parliamentary and other interests had evidently convinced the Committee that absenteeism, however distinguished the absentee, must have its limits). Within a year of Professor Kendall's appointment, and at his instigation, it was agreed by the Committee of Education that all First Senior students should be prepared for the Oxford Senior Local Examination, and all Second Senior students should be encouraged to take the Oxford Higher Local Examination. This recommendation appeared to counter the tradition of Queen's, which was averse to examinations, and suspicious of outside control. But times had changed, and qualifications were now a necessity for many women. Examinations were regarded as the criterion of the seriousness of an educational programme. The

Principal defended the decision in his Report to the Visitor in 1916:

> When the College was founded, such schemes of examination as then existed did not give much opportunity for instruction on true educational lines, and so submission to them meant, only too often, the neglect of real scholarship in the endeavour to acquire a sufficient elementary knowledge in a great many subjects in order to cover the ground prescribed; and so we feel that our founders were wise in refusing to recognise them.

But the modifications in examinations, and reduction in the number of subjects, would enable the College to teach for them

> without sacrificing our endeavour to impart true knowledge—a College tradition which we treasure most highly—yet at the same time to give proof to your lordship, and to all other friends of the College, that our students are at least as efficiently trained as other students of corresponding age.

Since that time the College has prepared its students for public examinations as a matter of course, but has yet never allowed the curriculum of either Juniors or Seniors to be dominated by their demands. As further evidence of seriousness, Professor Kendall arranged that the College day began at 9.30 instead of 10.0, so that seven lessons each of three-quarters of an hour could be fitted into the day, and the terms were made one week longer.

Professor Kendall resigned in 1918 and was succeeded as Principal by Joseph Edwards, the Professor of Mathematics. His lessons and lectures were difficult for those who had no flair for the subject, and to some he remained a remote figure. But so long as his health was good he was a full-time and very active Principal. That he had understanding and sympathy for the young is illustrated by the following story recounted by Dr Patricia Shaw:

7 Mrs S. C. P. Fierz, Principal since 1964,
on the stairs of No. 47 Harley Street
Photograph by John Adriaan

8 Mrs Fierz with the Prefects, December 1971,
on the stairs of No. 45 Harley Street
Photograph by John Adriaan

> One day my sister filched a carafe of water from her bedroom and crept to the Giraffe Hole intent on pouring the contents on any unsuspecting being walking below and then scuttling away. As she was getting into position for her nefarious deed, Professor Edwards, the Dean, emerged from his office (the room next the Principal's office, with the lead cistern over the fireplace). A moment later, there emerged from the other side of the landing a woman member of the staff who was a strict disciplinarian and was unlikely to show any sympathy for childish pranks. Professor Edwards got to my sister before she was seen and enveloped her in his gown. For hours and hours and HOURS a conversation about College affairs ensued, with Robina clinging to one of the Professor's legs and praying that the party would disperse before she sneezed. Finally the mistress went and all the Professor said was, 'Now don't do such a naughty thing again'. No wonder we called him 'Darling Joe'. I often wonder if the mistress noticed anything peculiar.

He was a delightful and very kind person and loved children. He used to walk round the preparatory department in the afternoons, and help the younger children with their sums, thus endearing himself to them. One former pupil of his says it was impossible to imagine him being angry.

Before coming to Queen's, he had been a lecturer in Mathematics at Wren's, then a famous coaching establishment, and had made his mathematical reputation with a series of books on Calculus. He adapted himself most successfully to the traditions and atmosphere of Queen's, and was a benevolent, if sometimes conservative, Principal of the College.

A new department was added to the College after the war, to match the advent of a new and socially acceptable profession for girls—the secretary. It was first suggested during the war, and a temporary arrangement was made for Queen's girls to attend the school of Miss Greig and Miss Gibson in Kingsway for a few hours a week. By 1919, the Committee of Education was ready to agree to secretarial studies being provided within the College itself. In that year Miss L. M. Dean was appointed to teach secretarial studies and to give secretarial assistance; she remained in the service of the College until her death in 1964. She created, nurtured and developed the secretarial department from the outset. The students who attended were given a professional secretarial training and prepared for the College certificate with outside examiners, while at the same time attending some of the academic lectures and classes of the College, thus receiving a broader training than they might have received at some other secretarial colleges.

The demand for courses in secretarial studies, domestic subjects, for preliminary medical instruction, and for the traditional academic subjects led the Principal in 1921 to present his suggestions for expansion to the Committee of Education. This was no doubt also prompted by the fact that the lease of 47 Harley Street, still the property of the Governesses' Benevolent Institution, was for sale. Four months later the College's offer to purchase the lease was accepted; what remained to be done was to raise the money. An Appeal Fund was launched, and after four years £10,000 had been raised—enough to justify the purchase and alteration of the house. It was first used in the autumn of 1925; on the ground floor the newly constituted Domestic Science department was housed, and on the first floor the main room was furnished as a comfortable and pleasant library (whose atmosphere of study remains impervious to the chatter which sometimes breaks its silence).

More than two years later, Queen Mary, the Patron of the College, visited Queen's to commemorate the extension of the buildings. In the December issue of the Magazine is the following description:

> Her Majesty had tea in the Library and was afterwards conducted to the Hall where Stephanie Tyacke, the youngest girl in the Hostel, presented her with a bouquet.

Stephanie Tyacke is now Mrs Fierz, the present Principal of the College.

Yet another extension was made in 1928. The landlords (the

Howard de Walden Estate) insisted on the rebuilding of the garage site in Harley Mews North, and so the opportunity was taken to build a gymnasium, a new studio and some extra classrooms. When these were opened in 1929 (by Princess Louise, Duchess of Argyll), the Hall no longer had to suffer callisthenics lessons, and the removal of wall bars and ropes to the nether regions was a great improvement. No longer did the porter have to go into the hall each morning to push all the chairs back against the wall ready for drill at break. The new studio was light and airy, and the earlier and less satisfactory studio had already been turned into a Biology laboratory. These additions improved but did not substantially change the buildings, and the old haunts, such as the Waiting Room, remained.

Gradually the masculine stronghold amongst the staff was being eroded, though not without some resistance. Before 1930, the management of the College was largely in the hands of the male professors, almost all of them part-time. Evidently in 1926, the Council suggested to the Committee of Education that the next Principal of the College might be a woman. The Professors replied that 'the suggestion is an unexpected one, but they are grateful for having it brought forward now, for it will ensure that no unconsidered decision is reached when the time comes for an appointment'. Two months after this letter was written, Miss G. E. Holloway was appointed the Senior Tutor; a year after her appointment, she deputised for the Principal when he was ill.[1]

Miss Holloway was an able and ambitious person. Her first teaching appointment was at Harrogate College, a modern well-equipped school with a good academic reputation. She wanted to see Queen's brought more up-to-date, to see more students going to university, and to see the facilities for science improved. She also wanted scope for her intellectual and organising ability. In 1928, the Council agreed to give her the title of Headmistress of the School and Vice-Principal of the College. In that year she

[1] Miss Holloway took the place of Miss Lewer, who had retired early because of illness and overstrain. Miss Lewer lived to be ninety-nine, and was still alive when this book was begun.

was the prime mover behind the rebuilding of the mews. But she still found the situation frustrating, especially the duplication of work between the Principal and herself. It was a great achievement when she persuaded the Council to agree to an inspection of the College and School by representatives of the Board of Education, against considerable opposition. It was an even greater achievement that after the death of Professor Edwards, she was appointed Principal. Professor Edwards died in 1931. For nearly a year, the Committee of Education and the Council procrastinated; 'they will appoint a woman over my dead body', one of the Council remarked to Miss Holloway, the Acting Principal. But the old order had to give way, and in March 1932 the Council appointed Miss Holloway as Principal; the Committee of Education also had the grace to say that 'there is no one with whom they could and would more cordially co-operate'. The opposition had come partly because of the inevitable masculine prejudice, which disappeared with time and experience; partly from one or two of the women members of staff who wished to retain the established tradition; and partly from old students for the same reason.

In 1928 the Rev H. F. B. Compston, Professor of Hebrew at Queen's, had written to the Principal:

> It almost seems as if the *force majeure* of changed conditions nowadays might necessitate the appointment of Women Professors; in English Literature especially I suppose there would be a wide choice of good candidates. But you have ever been a staunch upholder of Queen's College traditions—and they are well worth preserving if it may be so.

The traditions were preserved to the extent that no woman was ever given the title of Professor; but it was broken in that in 1932 Mrs Truman was appointed to take permanent charge of the teaching of Physics in both the School and the College, and was thus given the function without the status of a Professor. She was soon followed by others.

The Board of Education inspection took place in March 1931.

The purpose of the inspection, from the College's point of view, was to have Queen's recognised as 'an efficient secondary school'. This it was hoped would attract increasing numbers of students, and students of a higher standard. The Lady Visitors, whose function it was, until they ceased to meet regularly in about 1930, to award scholarships, were increasingly worried about the low standard of applicants for scholarships. One result of the inspection was indeed to secure 'recognition' from the Board. The other result, on the advice of the inspectors, was a considerable reorganisation of the College.

An inspectors' report is not always good source material for the historian. In this case, there are some useful and informative comments in the report. More valuable, perhaps, is the report of a meeting between the Inspectors and the Council. The Inspectors told the Council that they had been 'very much attracted and interested in their work during the week; an attraction which comes very largely from the kind of pupil that frequents the place'. This, we should hope, is still the case. They commented on the exceedingly generous ratio of student to staff of six to one.

Many people had already pointed out that this appeared wasteful in view of the financial difficulties in which the College frequently found itself. On the other hand, this is precisely the reason for many people's choice, in the 1930s and today, of an independent school for their children. They were particularly impressed with the standard of English; this was because of the work of Ernest Hockliffe (1922–7) and Arnold Taylor (1927–8), both retired masters of Uppingham, who inspired several students to study English at universities. The inspectors also received a good impression of the atmosphere of the place; and noted the favourable behaviour of the pupils and students.

The criticisms they gave were pertinent. The first was about salaries. There was by this time a Burnham scale, which applied to the salaries of all teachers in local authority schools. At Queen's the staff were paid 'much below the Burnham scale'. While there were still dedicated teachers who did not put the salary as their first priority, this might not be so in the future. About Miss Holloway, the chief inspector told the Council that they had 'actually got a lady doing what is not very far from being a Headmistress at half the salary of what a mistress of a Board Secondary School might hope to get'. As a result of the inspectors' comments, the salaries were raised, though not yet to the Burnham scale.

The other criticism was about the organisation of subjects, which was left too much to chance. No-one was really in charge of each department; the part-time Professors had not sufficient time, and no-one else was responsible. 'Everything has got to be tightened up,' said the inspectors. So a woman member of the teaching staff was appointed as the 'Head of Department' in almost every subject.

Another tradition which was disappearing was that of the Lady Visitors. During the First World War, they occasionally chaperoned lectures. After the war, chaperoning more or less ceased, and the Lady Visitors largely confined themselves to choosing scholars, and keeping an eye on them, expecting 'an earnest, standard of work'. Their last recorded meeting was in 1930. Just before this, they had been making the most of their opportunities, it seems, by arranging for the new Domestic Science department to cook them a special lunch on the day of their meeting. On December 9 1925 they recorded in their minutes:

> The Lady Visitors had asked that the Domestic Science students should provide and serve their luncheon. They requested that they might have a joint with a baked batter pudding and two vegetables, followed by a boiled apple pudding. They were disappointed to hear that Miss Walker wished to substitute an apple tart for the boiled pudding, as she considered it could not be cooked in time. The students begin their work at 9.30 and they would not be able to prepare anything beforehand as they were doing examination work earlier in the week. The Lady Visitors regretted that Miss Walker did not see her way to meet these difficulties and to supply the boiled pudding.

Miss Walker was asked to resign a few months later. She had certainly incurred the animosity of the Lady Visitors. By contrast, almost a year later, the Lady Visitors recorded that they

> sat down to a carefully laid table with a bowl of pink chrysanthemums in the centre and table napkins folded in the form of lotus lilies, and thoroughly enjoyed the appetising meal of four courses which was presented to them.

The menu was then listed and described in glowing terms. These lunches were continued after the era of the Lady Visitors, as good practice in entertaining for the very flourishing Domestic Science department.

During this period, as in the earlier years, students had considerable freedom, which some utilised and some abused. Some learnt remarkably little, but in the small classes, usually of fifteen or fewer, the best opportunities were given. One of the most interesting and remarkable of the students during the 1920s has vividly recorded her impressions of Queen's. Princess Sophie Dolgorouky came to England from Russia after the Revolution. Her mother decided that she would get 'more education and less games' at Queen's than anywhere else, and so she was entered for the School in 1919. A year later she wrote a horrifying, vivid description of the Revolution for the College Magazine. More recently she has written her autobiography, and recorded her reminiscences of the School:

> We were extremely fortunate in teachers imaginative enough to arouse enthusiasm for their respective subjects. I remember Miss Sutcliffe, young and pretty, who taught English and turned Shakespeare from the unbelievable stories of Lamb's Tales into a vibrating music. And Monsieur Cammaerts, with a flaming beard, who whacked your head with a ruler for mistakes in his beloved tongue or read aloud scenes from Molière, acting the various parts, or thundered out the magnificence of Racine. 'Gym' with Miss Lancaster, solidly built and dressed in a short gym tunic, who was somehow reminiscent of the Song of Solomon with her neck like an alabaster tower. Once a week there was dancing when we were taught how to

> reverse in a waltz and the difference between the one- and the two-step. For this we brought light frocks and slippers into which we changed. Every morning we filed in to the Hall for prayers and Roll Call taken by the Head, Miss Lewer, resplendent in hood and gown, and beside her the second-in-command, Miss Graham, who ruled the juniors and before whose steely eyes and high-piled hair one would be brought to account for one's various misdemeanours. There was a great variety of personalities at school, which was intoxicating after my heretofore rather solitary existence.[1]

These staff in the School were followed by others equally good. Miss Richardson was appointed to teach Science in 1927 and she was much admired; everyone wanted her good opinion. One cannot name them all. Professor Emile Cammaerts, who taught French in the College, was a great character with a considerable reputation outside the College.[2] When he gave a public lecture at the College in 1925 on 'The poetry of nonsense', the *Times* published a leader on it. Another later series of lectures he gave at Queen's was published.[3] When he resigned, the College Magazine remarked that no disciplinary measures had ever been taken in his classes—'none were ever needed, the Juniors were too awed to talk, and his Seniors far too interested'. He left in 1931 to become the first Professor of Belgian Studies at London University.

A second annual ceremony was added to the College year during this period. Annual Gathering was an old-established event; since 1854 (with a break between 1864 and 1881) the College students had been accustomed to gathering in white dresses adorned with flowers appropriate to their status in the College on a specified day in May to hear a visiting speaker. Since 1896 the speaker has always been the Visitor, that is, the Bishop of

[1] Sofka Skipwith, *Sofka. The Autobiography of a Princess* (1968), pp. 58–9.
[2] See Jeanne Lindley, *Seeking and Finding: the life of Emile Cammaerts* (1962).
[3] *Discoveries in England* (1930).

London, who shakes hands with each student before proceeding to the Pfeiffer Hall to address the students, some of their parents, and the staff. In 1926 the Bishop's speech was widely reported in the Press, though whether his advice was actually followed is doubtful. The *Evening Standard* reported it thus:

> 'If a young man takes you out to dine and offers you a cocktail, never go out with that young man again.' This was the Bishop of London's advice given to College girls at the annual gathering at Queen's College, Harley St, W. 'The secret of being young all your lives,' he emphasised, 'is "Don't drink; don't smoke, and take regular exercise".'

The second annual ceremony was Founder's Day, which was first held in 1928. It seems to have been originally the suggestion of Mrs Allport, a Lady Visitor, Council member, old student and parent, who was devoted to the College, as a way of raising money for the Appeal Fund. The first five Founder's Day services were held in Westminster Abbey, where special stalls had always been reserved for the Queen's boarders, presumably perpetuating a connection formed in the days of Dean Trench. Since 1933 the services have been held in St Peter's, Vere Street (where Maurice was Vicar from 1860 until 1869) in March of each year.

So Queen's moved into the 1930s, more modern, but still retaining the best of its individual traditions.

XIII

1932–45. Disaster Averted

By 1932 Queen's was beginning to resemble rather more closely the now well-established public day schools. The Principal and half of the Heads of Departments were women; the timetable included more lessons than lectures; and the students were prepared for examinations almost as a matter of course. Yet it never conformed entirely to the general pattern of girls' schools. There was still, and was to continue to be, a number of men professors; the students wore no uniform, and were not, on the whole, treated as schoolgirls; and the majority of students were over the age of sixteen. As late as 1940, the *Times* announced the appointment of a new Acting Principal under the heading 'University News'.

By this time, women had the vote on equal terms with men, and there were already women Members of Parliament. Many professions were now open to them. A 'serious' education for girls was more readily available, and more sought after.

Educational opportunities for girls had expanded. There were now grammar schools or high schools for girls, of good standard, all over the country. In London, there were numerous high schools, and public day schools such as St Paul's and the North London Collegiate School. There were boarding schools too, now very much sought after by middle- and upper-class parents for their daughters; not only the pioneer schools such as Cheltenham and Roedean, but a series of new foundations like Benenden (1923) and Westonbirt (1928). Queen's offered something in between: a day school, in the middle of London, with a separate boarding house attached.

During the 1930s Queen's suffered a decrease both in the numbers and in the quality of candidates for admission. There were constant complaints from the Committee of Education about the low standard of the scholarship entrants. Various reasons were considered by the Council. In 1935 Miss Holloway suggested to them that parents were now preferring a boarding school for their daughters; this theory was supported by the fact that many girls came as day pupils in the School and when they were old enough went on to a boarding school. Two years later, Sir Frederick Maurice, Chairman of the Council, suggested that the decrease was due to the decline in the birthrate, a factor affecting all schools. (In 1934, there were fewer children in Britain under the age of five than in 1871, though the population was twenty million greater.) He also suggested that the change in the character of the neighbourhood had something to do with it, with fewer people actually residing in the area.

It would be difficult to assess the reasons accurately. Very few girls' schools seem to have been founded in the 1930s, which suggests that the demands for independent girls' education were for the present time satisfied. In a time of economic depression, the comparatively high fees (£21 a term, with extras) may have discouraged some. It did mean that all the classes were small, and the students enjoyed considerable individual attention.

The largest department was the Domestic Science department, which formed two groups and had two full-time staff. The *Evening Standard* had written in 1928:

> The servant problem is altering the perspective of young society girls towards domestic work, and nowhere is their new attitude more evident than at the eighty-years old college, which has met modern conditions by the introduction of domestic science courses.

This course continued to flourish until the Second World War, and was revived again afterwards.

The Science department made a great step forward after the inspection of 1931. Mrs Truman, a part-time teacher at Queen's at a time when married women were excluded from all local authority schools, did as much as anyone to raise the standard, particularly in her own subject of Physics. Miss Richardson continued to inspire her pupils, and Miss Green came from the Herbarium at Kew to take late afternoon classes in Botany once or twice a week, until in 1938 she married T. A. Sprague, Deputy

Director of Kew. Both she and her husband were and are known internationally for their work on nomenclature in Botany. Many students came from outside to take a Science course with the Seniors, and all the able students were encouraged to go on to university.

Miss Holloway herself was very much interested in natural history and in walking, and she and Miss Green used to take nature rambles in the summer term, with Miss Holloway always leading the way. She also arranged, in 1939, for the pupils in the School to spend one day a week at a school in Beaconsfield, so that they could make a practical study of Geography and Nature Study.

The Boarding House survived, under the supervision of the Lady Resident (Miss Baird and then Miss Sherwood) and the same ritual and decorum continued. Students, however young were referred to as 'Miss' by the domestic staff. Each one had a private cubicle, to which maids brought hot water each morning. After breakfast in the Waiting Room and a walk, they took their places and spent the day amongst the day students. After tea and another walk they did some preparation and then changed into 'semi-evening dresses' for formal dinner in the Waiting Room. Each student sat where her napkin was placed, and was waited on and served in the three courses. In spite of the formality, the boarding students enjoyed themselves and did not have a solemn existence.

Miss Holloway and Pauline Merz, the senior student in 1933, started the prefect system and instituted the present weighted voting procedure for electing them; the vote of a member of staff or existing prefect to count for three, that of a Senior for two, and of a Junior for one. Only six prefects were appointed, such a small number that it did not induce feelings of failure in those who were not elected.

A new course was introduced about 1936 called a Modern Studies course; it still exists. It was intended for students of between sixteen and eighteen who wanted a one-year course of general studies after School Certificate. The course laid emphasis on literature and social studies and proved popular. Many students came into the College from other schools specially to take the course. One of the students who took part in this course in 1938–9 was Kathleen Kennedy, who was living in London because her father was American ambassador. She was later tragically killed in a flying accident.

Meanwhile the more academic work continued on the arts side as well as the science side, and there was a steady stream of girls going to university.

The 1930s were not particularly exciting years for Queen's. But good work was carried on, and the remark of one new student that the first thing that struck her was how kind everyone was has been echoed by many others.

By 1938 most people realised that a war with Germany could not be avoided much longer. Late that summer, the German occupation of the Sudetenland precipitated the Munich crisis. On September 28 there was an emergency meeting of the Council of Queen's. Possible places of evacuation were discussed; Lady Baldwin suggested asking Lord Rothschild whether he would lend his house at Tring to Queen's. But already Newlands, near Keswick, had been tentatively booked, and arrangements were hastily made for a departure. Most parents approved an evacuation for their daughters if the crisis continued, and plans were made for them to travel to Keswick via Euston on the morning of September 30. Eight hours before they were due to leave, the Munich agreement was announced. But the plans were so far advanced that the expedition left as arranged with fifty girls and several staff. For the next fortnight the College conducted its affairs in two places; in London, and in the Lake District. The Lake District party enjoyed themselves, appreciated the break in routine, and made the most of their opportunities for country pursuits and study. When they came back, they produced the *Newlands Journal*, a lively account of their adventure.

They all came back to London and the College was reunited. But the international crisis was only temporarily resolved, and peace was precarious. Miss Holloway began to look round for suitable places for evacuation. She found a house in Brackley, just inside the borders of Northamptonshire, and was able to book it at the end of May for occupation in case of war.

The international situation worsened throughout the summer.

In August, the last stages of diplomacy were being negotiated before the holocaust which everyone knew was imminent. On September 1, the general evacuation of schools and colleges from London took place. The parents of every student and pupil received a letter giving details of the travel arrangements to Brackley and of the required equipment:

> Every girl must bring health certificate, gas mask, mackintosh, goloshes or rubber boots; those in the Junior Years of the College and the School must wear uniform. Evening dress will not be required but every girl should have a warm afternoon frock.

Thirty-five students of the College and twenty-nine School pupils went to Brackley. (Those students who did not go to Brackley went to other schools, either in this country, the United States or Canada.) Miss Cartwright, Mayor of Brackley, had arranged the billets and staff and students were scattered all over the town. The headquarters were at Brackley House, but most of the lessons took place in rooms over an ironmonger's shop. Other neighbouring schools were generous in providing facilities; Stowe School provided science laboratories and so did Magdalen College School, and Brackley High School provided a gym and a domestic science kitchen. One student wrote in her Log Book that the headmaster of Magdalen College School 'takes the services in the chapel every Sunday which we go to if we are not in quarantine'. The full-time staff lived in Brackley, and the part-time staff travelled from London every week. The Magazine of January 1940 put the matter in a nutshell:

> The basement and Pfeiffer Hall of Queen's in London are now being used as a decontamination centre, and lessons and lectures are held in an ironmonger's shop in Brackley.

The A.R.P. were not entirely appreciative or respectful of the premises they were now occupying.

Every subject except Economics was taught, and Riding and Gardening were additions to the curriculum. 'Environmental studies' were part of the School timetable. While the weather was fine and warm, the pupils went for walks and talked to the people they met, to 'friendly ploughmen, thatchers of stack, threshers and other field workers'. When the weather grew colder, they went on visits to workshops, including 'a brewery, blacksmith's forge, farm, mill, cooper's workshop and a medieval castle'.

This arrangement continued until Christmas. Then came the most serious crisis in the history of Queen's. Certain members of the Council wanted the College to close. They felt that Queen's at Brackley made very poor comparison with other 'proper' boarding schools, and that no-one would want to send a daughter to school in the middle of London when air-raids were threatened. Without a reasonable number of students the College could not pay its way and there were no endowments, and few reserves.

A large number of the staff sent a petition against the closing of the College, and about six of them offered to receive only half the salary that was due to them, in order to help the College finances. Members of the Old Queen's Society were asked to contribute if they could to a fund to maintain the College in existence and many of them did so.

It was something of a venture of faith when the College re-opened in Harley Street on January 23 1940. The Council had agreed that the College might re-open in London, provided that there were at least five students. Four were found, three new ones and one from Brackley. What could be done? A hurried consultation between three members of the staff took place, and a fifth student was enrolled. Her name was placed on the register and her fees paid, but she never actually appeared because she herself knew nothing about it. The name of this fictitious student was in fact that of a private student, at home, of one of the three staff concerned. Years later, the niece of the private student whose name had been used, who did become a student at Queen's, was most puzzled to find her aunt's name down as a former student. Without this 'invention', it is almost certain that the College would not be in existence today.

The four students arrived at 47 Harley Street to begin the new term. They were ushered upstairs to the Library, where Miss

Dean talked to them for three-quarters of an hour about the history of the College. Then the classes began. Miss Dean stayed in London for the first half of the week, and Miss Kynaston for the second half, and both commuted to Brackley in between. Miss Holloway also commuted between the two colleges. Miss Oliver, officially the Principal's secretary, prepared the lunches at Harley Street. Other staff visited.

Within a few days, three more students appeared. These seven stayed for the term. The youngest was eleven, and alone constituted the School; she had private tuition. Three of them were about sixteen, but each one took a different course; secretarial, modern studies and I Junior. Another was twenty-five, and took the Senior Science course prior to taking up medicine. The last one was a Czech refugee in her thirties who came to study English. Variety and freedom were not sacrificed to the exigencies of war.

During that term, those who believed in the future of the College had to press hard. Lady Baldwin and Sir Frederick Maurice, in particular, gave Miss Holloway special support in the difficult Council meetings on the future of the College. Theodore Goddard, a parent and solicitor, offered financial support and wrote frequent pressing letters to the Council. In an optimistic spirit, special lectures were advertised on subjects like 'science in the modern world', Russian Literature, and French History and Thought, open to the public.

The Council had told Miss Holloway that they could not guarantee her salary after the end of the summer term. It was not surprising therefore that when she was offered the post of Principal of Alexandra College in Dublin, she accepted it, especially as it was the College founded by Archbishop Trench after the pattern of Queen's. She had served at Queen's for fourteen years, and had brought it up to date without allowing it to lose its essential atmosphere. She had from the beginning shown a special flair for choosing staff, and had built up a strong and happy team. Although a modest and unassuming person, she was an efficient organiser and had a capacity for pouring oil on troubled waters; she was no stirrer of controversies. It was a happy and loyal staff she left behind.

Miss Kynaston was immediately appointed Acting Principal. She had been at the College for only two years, but had already made her mark as an inspiring teacher of English and an efficient administrator. She also had courage and great perseverance, qualities which were soon to be put to the test.

Brackley House was closed at the end of the summer term. It was decided to continue the College with the forty-five students who were now coming to Harley Street; amongst them was Mary Churchill, who took time off to hear her father make his first speech in the House of Commons as Prime Minister. But Dunkirk had cast a dark shadow over the whole country and there was no knowing what the future had to hold.

The Battle of Britain began on August 13, when the Germans started their full-scale bombing attack on the south of England. By September 7, the main attack was being directed against London. Between that date and November 2, London was bombed hard every night, a process which produced resilience, stubbornness and courage rather than the gloom and defeat which were intended.

Queen's did not escape the suffering, though there was no direct tragedy. Miss Kynaston was the first to experience the rigours of the blitz. The night before her first staff meeting at the beginning of the Michaelmas term, her flat in Mecklenburgh Square was bombed and quite destroyed. Shaken but undeterred, she arrived by taxi in the early hours, and presided over the staff meeting later in the day as though nothing had happened. Queen's itself was blasted four times that term. On the first occasion, the buildings were temporarily unusable, though not seriously damaged. Equipment was piled into a taxi, and it and the students were directed to the Royal Academy of Music (Sir Stanley Marchant, a Council member, had promised such hospitality a few months earlier), where classes began at 10.15, just three-quarters of an hour late. They stayed for three weeks, until no 47 was made safe and habitable again. From then on, the raids became an accepted part of life. When the siren went, the A.R.P. opened the basement and most of the students went down there. A Hull tubular indoor shelter in the main corridor housed small classes. A contemporary, writing in the 1965 Magazine, remembered the 'indescribable noise' the students had to put up with while trying to continue studying:

> . . . hearty laughter and raucous jokes from the A.R.P., shorthand dictation and Latin declensions, punctuated by heavy thuds and vibrations as bombs fell, and occasionally the sinister whining of 'buzz bombs'—and through all this I remember sitting with a book of poetry on my lap and hearing Miss Kynaston say calmly, 'Try to concentrate on what Keats meant by the following lines—they are very important.'

Inevitably the raids affected the numbers. There were twenty-four names on the books for Michaelmas Term 1940. Of these, only fourteen put in an attendance of more than two or three days. (The School ceased to exist for the next two years.) Amongst these students was Sissel Lie, whose family had just escaped from the German occupation of Norway. Her father, Trygve Lie, was the Foreign Minister of the Norwegian Government in exile. Another sister spent a term at Queen's in 1942, and the third sister, who had to be left behind with her grandmother in Norway, came into the School in 1945.

The Battle of Britain was won by the spring of 1941 and the heavy raids on London virtually ceased. This made the daily life of Queen's somewhat easier, but did nothing to solve its financial problems. The numbers were creeping up only very slowly, with still only twenty students in the Michaelmas Term 1941. Each term threatened to be the last. It was not until 1942 that the accounts were balanced, and the immediate future seemed secure.

Meanwhile the Council was able to congratulate Miss Kynaston on the number of scholarships and university places. Founder's Day and the Clara Wood lecture were held for the first time for three years in 1942. And in the autumn of 1942, Miss Kynaston's temporary appointment as Acting Principal was changed into a permanent one as Principal. There were now sixty students.

The last crisis came with the flying bombs in 1944. The Council's prognostication on August 23 that 'it seemed very probable that the Flying Bomb menace would have largely if not entirely disappeared in the course of three or four weeks' was not unfortunately proved in practice, though the hurried plans made for an evacuation were not put into effect. Londoners learned to accept the threat which hung over them each day. School Certificate examinations were taken in the basement because of the raids. Seven staff had their homes damaged by raids, but were undeterred.

By the first months of 1945, there were 131 students at Queen's, and plans were made to go up to 170. After some discussion, it was decided that the College should remain in the existing premises, and negotiations were re-opened with the Howard de Walden Estate for the extension of the lease. Everyone felt that Queen's moved out to the suburbs, in however beautiful a setting, would not be Queen's, and Harley Street was so much its home. We have said earlier that most people would agree that the most important influence in any institution is that of the personalities, but that second to this comes the environment. Queen's has such an individual character that it really could not be the same in a purpose-built structure.

The other decision concerned the staff. Like many other independent educational institutions, especially those for girls which usually lacked endowments, Queen's paid its staff less than the standard Burnham scale which had been the accepted salary structure in all local authority schools since 1922. One does not have to assume that teachers, especially if they are single, will always be drawn to the highest-paid appointments. Queen's had been fortunate in having academically well-qualified staff with other qualities of personality who came because they liked the atmosphere, the individual attention which was possible in small classes, and the freedom from petty restrictions or cramping syllabuses. Some of the staff had shown great generosity during the war by going on to half salary so that the College could survive. But it would never be right to exploit such generosity, and in any case Queen's could not be unduly confident in hoping to continue to attract the best staff. So it was none too soon that the Council agreed, before the end of the war, to pay salaries according to the Burnham scale in future.

Nine staff worked for Queen's throughout the war, as well as Miss Kynaston. Miss Oliver was the Principal's secretary and turned her hand to any task which needed doing. She came to Queen's in 1932, acted as Principal's secretary for thirty-one years, and then became Registrar and Keeper of the College archives. She is now a mine of accurate information on the College history, and generously helps all researchers who come to Queen's in pursuit of F. D. Maurice, former staff or old students. Though not always in the public eye, Miss Oliver has always known more than most people of what was happening in the College. Miss Kynaston remarked in her valedictory report on Miss Oliver's 'remarkable memory for people and their activities, good and bad'.

Mrs Bailey did all the cooking for the College throughout the war. Her husband had been porter since 1934 and continued to live in the College basement flat until he died in April 1942. Mrs Bailey remained as cook and housekeeper until she retired in 1958. She was usually friendly and cheerful and even her complaining had an attractiveness of its own.

Miss Dean (known as 'secretarial Miss Dean' to avoid confusion with Miss Haslock Dean who had taught English before Miss Kynaston) continued to guide and inspire the Secretarial department. Loyalty to the College traditions was one of her guiding motives and she really came into her own on the two great days of the College year, Founder's Day and Annual Gathering. She had a wide range of interests, in art, history, and literature, and wove these skilfully into her teaching of secretarial skills. Social etiquette was another of her interests, and she delighted in teaching her students how to address (in writing) the younger son of an earl, or the elder daughter of a duke. When later on she retired from the teaching of secretarial subjects, she spent her time usefully in collecting and collating the College archives, and in keeping the records up to date. Each year she would address the new students and tell them about the history of the College. When she died, her friends, colleagues and old students endowed a lecture in her memory which was to be given every second year. The first one was given in the autumn of 1967 by the Archbishop of Canterbury on Maurice, and the second one by Clive Rouse in the spring of 1970 on English mediaeval wall paintings.

Mrs Truman continued to teach Physics throughout the war, and many of her old students then, as before and after the war, became eminent doctors or scientists. She had a very great influence on her group of science students, and set them a consistently high standard.

Mrs Bryson taught French to the English students, and English to the foreign students. She had been educated in France, and her sister, Violet Partington, was French tutor at Queen's for the first twenty years of the century. She was a charming and elegant person who interested and stimulated all her students. Other French classes had been taken by Maurice Thiéry, who spent part of his week teaching and part of it broadcasting to occupied France. Those whom he taught remember his 'exquisite French' and 'highly individual English'. After his death in 1947, the Principal wrote that 'his devotion to his work here when he was often worn out with grief and anxiety for his own country will not be forgotten'. His place was taken by another Frenchman living in London, Jean Parzy, a colleague of M. Thiéry at the B.B.C. who had also worked as a member of De Gaulle's staff in Carlton Gardens.

Miss Chaplin taught Latin throughout the war. She had once coached Miss Kynaston herself, and devoted her life to teaching her chosen subject. She was a born teacher, and spared no efforts to make the subject vivid and exciting. On the morning of D-day, she gave her students the story of the landing on the Normandy beaches in Latin for unseen translation; they could hardly believe it. She had written it hurriedly on the bus on the way to Queen's. When she was not teaching at Queen's, she was coaching at home. Miss Shewell-Cooper was another part-time teacher. Her subjects were English, Theology and 'Present-day problems'. She loved English Literature and passed on this love to her students. Later she was ordained as a Congregational minister (though still retaining her allegiance to the Anglican Church) and left Queen's after ten years of teaching there.

The last member of the staff who served Queen's throughout the war was Miss Mabel Floyd (Mrs Frederick Smith), who taught the piano. She was well-known in the musical world as a teacher and an adjudicator, and was devoted to her pupils. She was always smartly dressed, and made friends with everyone. Some of her pupils went on to be distinguished students at the London Colleges of Music. Miss Floyd never retired. She went on teaching past the age of 75, and finally collapsed and died within a very short time.

These staff exemplified the individuality and loyalty of so many of those who have taught at Queen's.

When the war ended, there were 131 students at Queen's. Plans were already being made for the centenary and for the expansion of the College. The Education Act of 1944 had provided for secondary education for all children. Was the future of the public schools assured?

XIV

1945–1964. Queen's After the War

QUEEN'S had survived the war by a hair's breadth. It now had to be built up afresh, to maintain its financial stability, and adapt itself to meet the needs of the post-war world. Miss Kynaston had the right blend of determination, enthusiasm and integrity to lead the College in these difficult years.

Miss Kynaston always exacted from herself and from others very high standards. This was partly because of her own innate character; but it owed something too to her own early background and struggle for education. She was the eldest daughter of a country vicar and was brought up in a family which accepted service to the community as its first duty. It was also a family in which money was short. There was not enough money to pay for the daughters to go to university. Mary, the eldest, stayed on at her own boarding school in Worthing as a pupil teacher; the next daughter took a Froebel training, and the youngest trained to be a nurse.

Mary Kynaston was not to be deterred by an obstacle such as shortage of money, and determined to gain a degree in her spare time. In 1928 she enrolled as a student at Birkbeck College and worked in the evenings and at week-ends for a B.A. Honours degree in English; this she was awarded in 1933. Not satisfied with this, she enrolled for a further degree, and spent four years preparing a thesis on *The life and writings of Charlotte Lennox.*[1] She used to go up to the British Museum on Saturday mornings to pursue her research. In 1937 she was awarded the degree of M.A. This interest in English Literature was something she retained throughout her life. After her retirement she continued research into drama history, and at the time of her death she was preparing an article for a scholarly journal.

[1] Charlotte Lennox (1720–1804) was a novelist and author of *Shakespeare illustrated* (1753–4).

Her former students all remember her as a brilliant and inspired teacher of English. She was able to convey her own enthusiasm for the subject, and the weekly classes on 'The History of Drama', which all I Senior Arts attended, were very much enjoyed.

Another great interest was librarianship. Miss Kynaston was one of the earliest members of the School Library Association, and served as secretary of the London branch for many years. She took a great interest and a great pride in the Library at Queen's. She also ran the Junior Library for the School herself. She loved books and loved looking after them; she was meticulous about detail herself and trained others to be the same.

One of the most important tasks of a Principal is to choose her staff. Here Miss Kynaston had a flair for choosing people who were enthusiastic about their subjects, ready to work hard (as everyone had to), and who proved to be interesting and congenial personalities. Having chosen them, she gave them the freedom to do the job as they thought best.

This staff worked together happily throughout these years. Many of its members agreed that it was the happiest staff room they had known. Part of the reason lay in the freedom given to each member of staff and the comparatively small amount of regulation which had to be imposed. This of course is only possible in a small school, where everyone can be known to everyone else, and where arrangements and decisions can be made through personal contact rather than through written rules and documents. Another reason was the personal interest which Miss Kynaston took in the staff and in their families and the understanding she showed in their difficulties. And yet another reason was the understanding and tact shown by the three members of staff who acted as Senior Tutors during these years.

It was the task of the Senior Tutor to do a certain amount of administration, such as helping with the timetable, arranging examinations, and organising staff duties. It was also her task to act as a sort of liaison officer between the Principal and the staff, and here she could make or mar the relationship. In each case, the Senior Tutor created a happy and friendly atmosphere.

Mrs Marjorie Sharpe (later Mrs Shipp) came to Queen's during the war as History Tutor, and stayed for seven years. During that time she maintained the standard of History teaching at a high level and inspired many students to continue their study at university. As Senior Tutor she brought a warm, kind and mature influence to bear in the staff room, at the same time enlivening it with her keen sense of humour. After her second marriage she left in 1950 to spend more time at home. She died in 1968.

Her successor as Senior Tutor was Miss Meg Graves, who had joined the staff in 1946. She brought a lively and enthusiastic approach to her teaching of Classics and Classical Background, and there was nothing dull about her lessons. She was a gay, friendly and efficient Senior Tutor who took all crises in her stride and enlivened the staff room with her infectious humour. She resigned in 1955 to teach in Sweden, but before going announced her engagement, and returned home to become Mrs Parker.

In 1955 Miss Beatrice Burstall became the Senior Tutor and remained in this position until 1965. Miss Burstall first came to Queen's in Michaelmas 1949 as a part-time Tutor in Theology and became full-time Tutor the following term. In that capacity she has had a remarkable influence over several generations of students, providing theological teaching of an unusually high academic standard, and combining tolerance with strong personal religious conviction. As Senior Tutor she showed many personal kindnesses to members of staff and to students which were unknown to others, and smoothed out many a potentially difficult situation.

The staffing ratio at Queen's was high compared with the majority of schools, and part-time members of staff came in to take small classes or individuals. This may have been uneconomic and expensive but it meant that individual programmes could be made for each girl, providing a wide choice of subject. It was still possible to register as a non-compounder, taking one or two subjects only.

Most of the part-time staff combined their teaching at Queen's with work outside. Mademoiselle Blondeau, for example, taught

French at Queen's during the day, using what one of her former pupils has described as 'inimitable teaching methods', and adults at evening classes later on in the day, using the intervening hours to correct the innumerable corrections and re-corrections of her younger pupils.

The programme provided in the School was a four-year course, starting with Class Four and working up to Class One. Entrants to Class Four were normally ten years old (the preparatory classes were not started again after the war). This class was taken largely by one person. The other three classes of the School were taught by several members of the staff, most of whom also taught in the College. Each class contained on average about twenty pupils.

At the age of fourteen or so, the Class One pupil moved into the College, into the I Junior year. This meant moving from a classroom in the School corridor into a room next to the office near the front door. It also meant shedding uniform, and experimenting with fashion. Occasionally startling experiments were made, but most students soon settled down and the general standard of dress was good. For the first two years of the College, in the I and II Junior, the work was preparation for School Certificate, or after 1950, G.C.E. Ordinary Level.

After this stage had been reached, there was a choice of courses open to each student. The normal academic courses were provided for Higher School Certificate (later G.C.E. Advanced Level), and University Entrance, in a Senior Science group and a Senior Arts group. At this point, a number of girls aged about sixteen came from other schools to take these courses.[1] Some of them came from small boarding schools which could not provide anything beyond Ordinary Level; some of them were not prepared to stay at boarding school any longer and wanted a day school; some of them had got across their school authorities (like the girl who was described by her previous headmistress as 'tiresome, turbulent and talkative') and wanted to make a fresh

[1] Immediately after the war, there were also much older students who had been in the Services and now wanted to make up for lost time.

start. This mixture of students who had come up through the School and College and students from elsewhere was very stimulating but it did call for a great deal of flexibility and hard work on the part of the staff, and since the background of each student might be different, the academic standard was inevitably sacrificed a little. This was especially true of Science, for some students embarked on an Advanced Level Science course without having done any disciplined study in Physics and Chemistry before. It was a hard task to reach Advanced Level standard in three Science subjects in two years, and it was remarkable that so many students were able to do so.

Mrs Truman continued to teach Physics until her retirement in 1968, interesting and stimulating both scientists and non-scientists in her subject. Miss Lambert came in 1946 to teach Biology and her lively and efficient teaching has been a valuable part of the Science education at Queen's. A student of a particularly naughty form in the 1950s remembers 'the Biology lessons which we used to love and never stopped asking Miss Lambert a stream of questions, seldom about the subject we were actually working on, and which she always answered'. The laboratory equipment was not as up-to-date as the staff would have liked, but there was no money for expensive improvements. However, a grant from the Industrial Fund for the Advancement of Scientific Education in Schools did enable the College to buy some new equipment for the Physics and Chemistry laboratories.

The work on the Arts side was not under quite the same pressure because any girl wanting to take an Advanced Level course would almost certainly have studied that subject before. The opportunity to give a broad education without narrow confinement to examination requirements was taken. In English, for example, the I Senior course included lectures on the History of Drama, and a course on Modern Literature, and only in the II Senior year were the required set-books studied in detail. A steady stream of girls was prepared for University Entrance in almost all subjects.

The one-year Modern Studies course was continued and usually included at least twelve students. They took some lessons and lectures with the I Senior Arts and some on their own.

Three other courses were available. The Secretarial department under Miss Dean (until 1956) continued to offer a one-year course. The Domestic Science department under Miss McVicker (until 1960) also offered a one-year course. And the course for foreign students was continued, with a mixture of English Language teaching and English History and Literature. Girls of many different nationalities came to do this course, but it seemed particularly to attract Japanese girls, who made up for their lack of fluency in the English Language by their charm, poise and hard work.

The practice of arranging general lectures by visiting experts was continued. Every Wednesday afternoon in the Michaelmas and Lent terms, the Seniors gathered in the Pfeiffer Hall to hear a lecture on art, social service, travel or some other subject. Robert Harris and John Laurie gave enthralling poetry readings. There were numerous societies too. A debating society met every week, and sometimes debated with another school. When Miss Greenslade came to Queen's in 1946 to teach Music, she founded the Music Club, which has flourished ever since. In 1957 the Music Club celebrated its tenth birthday—'a most happy occasion—not at all damped by the last moment realisation that it should have been held a year earlier'. Miss Greenslade has been tireless in arranging and taking part in visits to concerts and operas and has given encouragement to hundreds of musicians at Queen's, both amateur and intending professionals.

One unusually named society has organised some enterprising and interesting meetings. The Catacombs began in 1955, when a group of Seniors expressed enthusiasm for discussion of religious problems. A passing remark by a member of staff, who thinking an esoteric society was hatching, compared it to the Catacombs, led to the name, on the principle of *lucus a non lucendo*, being immediately adopted. Interest in the group has waxed and waned with each generation of Seniors, but the standard of speakers has remained consistently and remarkably high. Amongst notable talks were one on 'Buddhism' by the Rev George Appleton, another on 'Religion and Science' by Dr

Roger Pilkington, one on 'Christianity and Communism' by Canon Douglas Rhymes, and another on 'Prayer' by Archbishop Anthony Bloom. These are only examples and there have been many other lecturers of distinction. These meetings were made possible partly by Miss Burstall's own wide interests and contacts, and partly by the remarkable willingness of such busy people to give up their time to talk to this group.

Sport did not play as large a part in the life of Queen's as in other girls' schools. This was due mainly to the lack of facilities. It was quite a long walk up to Regent's Park to play games, or to the Seymour Place Baths for swimming, and as much of the lesson was spent walking as playing or swimming. But fencing tuition was provided in the College, and Queen's was very proud of Gillian Sheen, a former student, who won a Gold Medal for fencing in the Olympic Games in 1956. Every Senior had to attend a lesson in the gym once a week, still dignified by the original name of 'callisthenics'.

The tradition of social service was continued, in collections for charities and particularly in practical help to the Lady Margaret Hall Settlement in Lambeth. The link with this settlement went back to the end of the nineteenth century when Edith Langridge[1] (student at Queen's 1881–5) was its first Warden, and Lucy Hodson (student 1885–9) her assistant. Girls arranged parties and entertainments for invalid children, and later for old people as well.

College celebrations were revived after the war and still continue. Founder's Day was celebrated in the Lent Term each year, as before, with a service in St Peter's, Vere Street. Annual Gathering came in the Summer Term. The Bishop of London, as Visitor, continued the custom of shaking hands with each girl as she stood in the main corridor wearing her white dress adorned with the flower appropriate to her year, before going into the Pfeiffer Hall for the speeches (but no prizes).

In 1948 the College centenary was celebrated. Tradition was

[1] She later became Mother of the Oxford Mission Sisterhood of the Epiphany in India.

upheld by a much-appreciated visit by the Queen (now the Queen Mother). The whole College and School shared an enormous ceremonial cake shaped like a book with pages of Queen's history in it. A centenary history[1] of the College was published, written by Lady Mander, formerly Rosalie Glynn Grylls, a student at Queen's 1919–23. A series of lectures was given on distinguished old students and professors of Queen's. Lieutenant Colonel Tarrant gave a lecture on Dorothea Beale, whom he remembered. Robert Sterndale Bennett gave a lecture on his grandfather, William Sterndale Bennett. Canon Charles Raven gave a lecture on Maurice. And there were others. A dramatic adaptation of Tennyson's *The Princess* was given by the College Dramatic Society. An interesting centenary exhibition was mounted, comparing the life of the student of 1848 with that of her counterpart in 1948. It was an interesting and imaginatively conceived programme.

In 1953, another celebration was arranged for the centenary of the granting of the Royal Charter to the College. A dinner was held in the Hall of the Grocers' Company, of which Major Dent, Chairman of the Council, was a past Master, and the speakers were Janet Dunbar, the Bishop of London and Peter Noble, Principal of King's College, London.

Other occasions for celebration were taken regularly. At Christmas a party was given for both the School and the College. In 1952, the pupils and students were handed a programme for a pantomime called 'Queen's Rhapsody, or Flora and Fauna', with a somewhat strange-looking cast list. They were taken utterly by surprise to realise that Belle FitzRector, taking the part of a fairy, was really Miss McVicker, that B. Rumpototus, reading the Prologue, was really Miss Burstall, and that all the other curiously named members of the cast were in fact members of the staff.

The School and College drew girls from a wide variety of backgrounds. As with all independent schools, some came from families who could afford most things they wanted; others came from families who had to make real sacrifices in order to pay the

[1] Rosalie Glynn Grylls, *Queen's College 1848–1948* (1948).

fees. The fees inevitably had to rise steeply in order to meet the increasing salaries of the Burnham scale.

Miss Kynaston wanted to attract girls who valued the education which she and her staff had to offer. There were no endowments, and though there were several scholarships, the monetary value was small.

The *Sunday Times* for July 22 1956 mentioned a forthcoming debate on education in the House of Commons, and said that it might 'provide another occasion for some Member to put in a plea on behalf of middle-class parents for tax relief on school fees'. It went on:

> This relief has been refused so far, but a new suggestion from the head of a well-known girls' public school offers an ingenious yet simple alternative which obviates the objection of direct help to one section of the community.
>
> The idea comes from Miss A. M. Kynaston, Principal of Queen's College, Harley Street, London. She proposes that all parents of children of secondary school age should be given vouchers of the annual value of the cost of secondary education in State schools. Every term the parent would hand to the school of his choice a coupon representing a third of this amount.

Nothing has yet come of this idea, but it has been seriously suggested from several quarters since.

One new scholarship has been endowed since the war, the Florence Scholarship, after a gift of £10,000 from Miss Ernestine Florence, an old student, in 1957. Miss Kynaston remarked in the *Annual Report* for that year that this was 'the first and only large sum of money the College has received in the one hundred and nine years of its existence'. Even then, the regulations of the scholarship were very restricting.

The variety of background was much more than a matter of economics. Amongst the girls at Queen's there has been for a long time a number from Jewish homes.[1] After the war, the

[1] There were Jewish girls at least as early as 1865.

proportion in the School and College together was about a quarter. This situation, in a College founded by clergymen of the Church of England, in which religious teaching has always played an important part, called for considerable sympathy and understanding. This has for the most part been forthcoming, and the Christians and Jews have been encouraged to respect each other's religious heritages and convictions. It is a Jewish former student who has written, 'I think aside from her academic standing, Miss Kynaston's great gift to Queen's was her own tolerance and religious conviction.'

In the School and I Junior all the girls have studied the Old Testament together for one lesson a week, and then the Christians have had in addition one New Testament lesson a week. In the II Junior and the Senior years, Theology[1] usually occupied one period a week, and was optional for non-Christians. On one day a week, joint prayers were said in the morning assembly; on the remaining four days, the Jewish girls had their own separate prayers, taken by Miss Blumenthal, a German teacher who had escaped from Hitler's persecution in the 1930s, and who has shared many intellectual and practical interests with her students since she came to Queen's in 1943.

Not only were there Jewish girls, but girls of other religions, including Buddhists and Muslims from many parts of the world. The roll call after prayers each morning contained some fascinating and hitherto unheard-of names, and these girls' dress added colour and interest to the daily life. One former student has said that life at Queen's 'was an exercise in learning to live with people of different races, religious persuasions, mental and physical capabilities.'

Queen's still occupied the same building as the first students

[1] This is the word used by Maurice to describe the subject. In his Inaugural Lecture he stated: 'We would have avoided a hard word if we could; but if we had substituted religion for theology, we should have misrepresented our whole scheme. We look upon all the studies of which I have spoken as religious; . . . By theology, we mean something special and definite; we mean, what the word expresses, that which is directly concerned with God and His relation to man.'

of 1848. In 1954 numbers 43, 45 and 47 Harley Street were scheduled as buildings 'of special architectural or historic interest' and they cannot now be materially altered without permission. Meanwhile their surroundings were changing. During the war the houses opposite were bombed, leaving a derelict site to be used later as a car park. In 1959 plans were announced for a large garage on this site. Opposition to this was immediate and vociferous, with Queen's playing its full part. After wrangling and litigation the plan was eventually quashed and instead a large block of flats was built. The final result was seemly and in character with the neighbourhood, but the process of building, which took a matter of years, proved a nightmare of pneumatic drills and general noise for those trying to concentrate on teaching or learning on the east side of the building.

There was never quite enough room in the three houses in Harley Street. Apart from this, there were frequent requests from parents for a weekly boarding house. In 1960 discussions began about the possibility of taking over the lease of 49 Harley Street. This was made possible in 1962, and the house came into use in the autumn of 1963. The ground floor housed the secretarial department and the archives; the first floor provided a most suitable additional room for the Library; and the rest of the house was used as a weekly boarding house with a resident warden. This house was later most appropriately named Kynaston House. Miss Kynaston had used her ingenuity to devise ways of raising money to help to acquire the house, and had taken immense trouble with its planning and redecoration; the result was evidence of her own good taste.

The room which the Secretarial department vacated on the first floor of no 45, the original room in which Maurice and his friends lectured, was restored to its original form and redecorated, and furnished as a music-room and small lecture-room. It was named the Floyd Room, in memory of Mabel Floyd, for it housed the piano which she had left to Queen's.

Miss Kynaston announced her resignation in the autumn of 1963. In her last but one Annual Report she gave a summary of the kind of education she had tried to practise during her career. In it, her former pupils will recognise a familiar voice and ideal:

> The demoralising trends of the present way of life make it obvious that still, as always, the responsibility of character training is the most important part of true education. We hope that the acquisition of number 49 and the work and activities we shall be able to plan will strengthen our power to build characters strong enough to counter the prevalent passivity with mental and spiritual effort; the expectation of being entertained with the capacity to entertain oneself and others; the superficial knowledge of today with some genuine scholarship; selfishness with a desire for service; shifting standards with some absolute values. If we can achieve something of this at Queen's even our small community will have its contribution to make in the future, as it has in the past, to the ultimate good of the community at large.

It stands as a good testimonial to her career.

She retired at the end of the summer term in 1964. She found plenty of occupation for herself, both in London and in the Dorking home where she had loved to entertain her students, past and present. She took the opportunity to travel more than she had been able to do before. She carried on an extensive correspondence with some of her former students and staff and continued to welcome them to her home. It was with great sadness that her friends, and former colleagues and students heard that she had been killed in a road accident in May 1970. They knew she would not have taken kindly to a long and declining old age; but she died when she still had so much to contribute.

Miss Kynaston's successor as Principal—Mrs Stephanie Fierz—was appointed in February 1964. Mrs Fierz was well qualified to lead Queen's. She was an old student, a former member of staff, and mother of a student. The Council could be sure that she would understand and appreciate the traditions of Queen's. At the same time, she had had plenty of experience of schools very different from Queen's, both in England and abroad, and was not likely to ignore, in the interests of tradition, the good developments taking place in education as a whole.

Queen's now prepared to move forward under a new Principal to the years ahead.

XV

Queen's Today

SINCE 1964 life at Queen's has followed a busy and interesting course. What changes most conspicuously is fashion. Hemlines move up and down with alarming rapidity; it would be difficult to find a better vantage point for studying the height and breadth of fashion than the main corridor at the end of the afternoon. But the atmosphere remains the same. Annual Gathering and Founder's Day are still celebrated, the same mixture of nationalities and religions learn to live together, and the 'right of talking' is still vociferously upheld.

The new Principal is a scientist and has made sure that the teaching of both arts and science subjects keeps abreast of modern developments. The scientific laboratories were becoming overcrowded because of the increased demand for Advanced Level courses in Science. In 1969 plans were made for building a new Science block in the Domestic Science department, whose small numbers hardly justified their taking up so much space. A new Chemistry laboratory was finished in 1970, and a new Physics laboratory was planned for the near future. This was made possible primarily because of a most generous gift of £10,000 by Mrs Merz, in memory of her daughter Pauline, who was Senior Student in 1933 and was later killed in an air raid; there were other generous smaller gifts. With Mrs Truman's resignation in 1968, an era in scientific education at Queen's came to an end; for thirty-eight years she had so effectively presided over the Physics laboratory.

Miss Burstall resigned as Senior Tutor in 1965 and retired as Tutor in Theology in 1968. She was succeeded as Senior Tutor by Miss Lambert who, as the Principal said in her Annual Report, 'has a marked tendency to do and get things done at least a fortnight before it is necessary'. She has provided a most efficient organisation for the running of the College, and has set an example of conscientious and unfailing diligence.

The artistic, musical and dramatic life of the College has been lively and enterprising. Queen's has taken part in several dramatic and operatic performances with boys from Westminster School, ranging from Oscar Wilde's *The Importance of Being Earnest* to Samuel Becket's *PLAY*. The most *avant-garde* of the cultural activities have been the performances of David Bedford's music under his own direction; small groups of girls have met together weekly to play 'experimental music' and have given performances of it in different centres in London.

The number of students applying for university entrance has increased considerably, and the present uncertainty about the role of the university in modern society is reflected, in miniature, at Queen's. Those who want to continue their education tend to think that university education is the only kind worth having, and so some students apply who would perhaps find other kinds of further education more suitable and satisfactory. On the other hand, many of those whose teachers consider them suitable have to show determination and wait two years before they gain a place because of the shortage of places and the rather unsatisfactory methods of selection used. Everyone agrees that the outstandingly able find places, and that the totally unsuitable are rejected; but in between there are so many candidates with reasonable qualifications who do not always seem to receive equitable treatment, for whom university application is a form of lottery.

Academic and cultural activities take precedence at the College, with sport commanding increasing enthusiasm, but social service is not forgotten. A branch of Task Force, an organisation founded by the brother of an old Queen's student to enable and encourage the young to help the elderly, has found considerable support and is run by the students themselves. The Principal has joined groups of students in the present fashionable but profitable sponsored walks in aid of Shelter and other charities. An annual drive to raise money for social service challenges the ingenuity of each Year; the boldest idea, which found three willing collaborators, was to place members of the staff in the stocks and charge 6d a time for the privilege of throwing a wet sponge at them.

Queen's is still very proud and sensible of its history and traditions, though not, one hopes, allergic to change. Portraits of Maurice still hang in the main corridor and the Library, and one is reminded of his statement at the opening of the College, 'we shall be glad to improve our practice every day, not to alter our principle'.

It is now a hundred years since Maurice died. His ideas, his ideals and his integrity still leave their mark. He would not have wished to be put on a pedestal. But he was a rare human being with prophetic insight, and his integrity shines brightly in a world clouded and distracted by competitiveness, materialism and self-seeking, a world tempted to reach for easy, though often expensive, means of escape.

The students of today have to learn to take their place in a rapidly changing world. They may well combine a professional career with marriage and raising a family, and may find that retraining is necessary within their own professions. The best preparation for this is surely to be taught and challenged to think. Maurice said in his inaugural lecture:

> . . . the teachers of a college must lead their pupils to the apprehension of principles. . . . When I speak of leading our pupils to the study of principles, I think I mean something as nearly as possible the opposite of introducing them to an encyclopaedia of knowledge.

This is the kind of teaching which is ultimately the most rewarding, but its practice takes a considerable amount of courage in a world in which success is so often judged by examination results alone. The present Principal has allied herself firmly on Maurice's side. In the Annual Report for 1965–6 she stated:

> In these days of cut-throat competition for entrance to Universities, and indeed to any further training, it is tempting to regard our main function to be the acquisition of qualifications. I submit that this should be less so than ever before . . . One might almost say that our main function is to teach people to teach themselves; to open the door to what should be a life-long development.

Queen's has always provided a liberal and unrepressive atmosphere. This is partly because it has always had more students in the College than in the School—more girls over fourteen than below. It has made it more natural to treat them all as students rather than as schoolgirls. Because it is a comparatively small College it is possible to consider each student's timetable individually, and to allow any combination of subjects to be studied. The incentive to work is not bolstered up by rewards and punishments, and the result is that hard work is the norm. Naturally there are backsliders, but they are not typical, and when finally they do decide to work, it is because of their own decisions.

Queen's is a small, independent, single-sex school, not the kind of educational establishment fashionable at the moment. Yet it continues to flourish. What does it give its students which makes parents want to send their daughters there? If social snobbery forms any part of the reason, this had no part in the intentions of the founders, and is not encouraged or fostered by the staff. We have seen throughout its history that Queen's has set no stamp or mould upon its students and has not presented an image to which everyone is expected to conform. It has always set out to discover and develop the individual gifts and aptitudes of each person, to provide an atmosphere in which students may be free to be themselves at their best. In an age in danger of cultivating mediocrity and conformity this is refreshing.

The purpose of the College (and School) is education. Education is not a solemn or dull activity, but a lively and stimulating one, a process which teachers and students can enjoy together. At the same time, they should have a common aim—the pursuit of truth. Maurice's last words in his inaugural lecture still holds good: 'If this College cannot stand upon the condition of its teachers continuing to be honest men, by all means let it fall.'

INDEX

INDEX